THE FIVE LAWS OF STILLNESS

A Rebel's Guide to Spiritual Unfoldment

JESSICA AYALA

Copyright © 2024 Jessica Ayala All rights reserved

No part of this book may be reproduced, or stored in a retrieval system, or transmitted in any form or by any means, electronic, mechanical, photocopying, recording, or otherwise, without express written permission of the publisher.

Cover design by: Jessica Ayala
Copyediting: Erin Gahan Clark

Library of Congress Control Number: 2018675309
Printed in the United States of America

The Highest Thought Publishing
P.O. Box 361
Skyland, NC 28776

www.jessicaayala.com

To my little girl, Chloe - our first love.
I feel you with me everyday.

To my boys -
Your light is the most magnificent brilliance I've ever
known.
Thank you for sharing it with me.

"Somewhere on this journey the human consciousness or intellect, comes to a place where it gladly bows to its spiritual self and confesses that this spiritual self is Christ, is highest, and is Lord."

Emilie Cady

TABLE OF CONTENTS

Prologue

Part I - An Introduction to Stillness

    Chapter 1: My Inner Rebel

    Chapter 2: At Some Point in History

    Chapter 3: The First Law of Heaven

    Chapter 4: The Space Between Movement

Part II - The Five Laws of Stillness

    Chapter 5: The Law of One-Mindedness

    Chapter 6: The Law of Creating Space

    Chapter 7: The Law of Co-Creation

    Chapter 8: The Law of Celebration

    Chapter 9: The Law o Nonresistance

    Chapter 10: The Light That is You

Afterword

Glossary of Terms

Mantras of The Highest Thought

Acknowledgement

About the Author

PROLOGUE

When I began writing this book, I knew it wasn't meant to be another guide to physical stillness. Mostly because my deepest moments of peace didn't come from sitting in quiet solitude; they emerged from surrendering to loving presence, guided by the voice of Spirit within. This understanding revealed to me that true stillness is not merely about being motionless, but about aligning our perceptions with a higher consciousness of love—a force I refer to interchangeably as Christ Consciousness, Higher Consciousness, The Universe, the Holy Spirit, God, or the Divine. This life-affirming presence exists beyond the confines of time, and when we attune ourselves to its rhythm, stillness naturally becomes the *truth* of who we are.

Truth, as commonly understood today, is derived from Old and Middle English, connoting accuracy, righteousness, and faithfulness to religious doctrine. However, in its earliest Hebrew form, emet (אֱמֶת), truth encompasses a broader understanding—a wholeness that endures from beginning to end, eternal and all-knowing. Further back, in Proto-Indo-European (PIE), the root of the word Truth (deru) was shared with the word tree, both symbolizing firmness, unwavering, and steadfastness.

It is these early, all-encompassing definitions of truth—firm, solid, and enduring—that guide this book. And while stillness in a physical sense can realign us with the *truth* of our being, aligning with higher consciousness is equally available when navigating the chaos and uncertainty of life, when facing feelings of inadequacy, lack, or worry about the world.

In many ways, the ability to cultivate unwavering stillness is a lost art, which is why I felt compelled to write this book. I needed the principles within to help me navigate my own perceptions while grappling with fear in the form of depression, overwhelm, and especially anger. For a period in my adult life, anger was a dominant force, leaving me feeling like I was constantly failing. This book is a reflection of the spiritual truths that helped me realign with stillness and heal emotionally. To this day, I return to these lessons in moments of impatience, when I crave peace but can't find quiet, when I forget how to surrender what is out of my control, or when I simply want to remember the essence of my badass self again.

Having made mistakes, faced trauma, and walked difficult paths, I've learned that stillness isn't always found in silence or solitude. It arises when we embrace life in its fullness—grief, joy, and all the spaces in between.

While many of my experiences are shared throughout these pages, there are two key memories that did not make it in the book but have lingered in my mind. Perhaps because they are personal struggles that represent crucial moments where inner peace did not come from the absence of movement, but from spiritual surrender.

The first memory is from when I divorced my first husband, who was from the Czech Republic. I met him when I was 21, and he was 10 years older. I never truly wanted to be with him, but he pursued me relentlessly during one of the loneliest times of my life —when I was on my own, barely getting by in Nashville, TN. He would show up unexpectedly at my job, call me constantly, and eventually convinced me to move in with him. After two years together, we eloped at a courthouse in Kentucky. I was heartbroken that day. I didn't tell my family because I didn't love him in that way. Though there wasn't physical abuse, it was a manipulative relationship, and I felt trapped with a sense of obligation to him. I ignored countless intuitive messages that urged me to get out. Instead, I kept trying to force peace and love in a relationship that was incompatible, coerced, and toxic.

One night, as I was driving home in tears, seeking guidance on my situation, I was awakened by a whisper that asked *why was I so insistent on living a life that wasn't meant for me?* The moment I heard this thought, my internal world shifted. I realized I had been keeping myself a prisoner in a life I didn't want. I also realized that my marriage reflected the toxic and confining relationships I had witnessed growing up. This realization was one of the first times I consciously recognized how we, as humans, can unconsciously keep ourselves stuck in detrimental environments or repeat generational patterns simply because they feel familiar.

Acknowledging this truth, grieving the familiar suffering, and opening myself to the unfamiliar feelings of love and the potential for an aligned relationship marked the moment when peace began to return to my life. This revelation led me to finalize my divorce and write a lengthy letter declaring what I desired in a future partner. Three months later, I met my current husband, who embodies every word of that letter.

The second memory is one of the most painful for me—the loss of our baby girl, Chloe. I was five months pregnant when we lost her. Shane, now my husband, and I had only been together for a year when I found out I was expecting. The grief that followed her passing was indescribable. In the hospital, before I delivered her, we played music for her, placing headphones on my belly. We told her how much we loved her; how much we would miss her. When she was born, we held her and cried. The pain was overwhelming, and at one point, the nurses offered to medicate me. But again, I heard a thought that was not my own, given to me as instruction: *Be here now— in love and in grief*. I obeyed, choosing to feel every ounce of the pain and to face the heartbreak head-on. In that surrender, I found stillness.

I share these stories to set the tone for what follows. So often, how we navigate life—whether healing, coping, or creating—is shaped by our past or by societal pressures to conform or dismiss suffering, and even to stifle joy. But I've learned that reclaiming the lost art of true, lasting stillness arises when we turn toward life, embracing both joy and sorrow as they come, and trusting that love, in its purest form, is always present to guide us forward when we are willing to receive that guidance.

In the chapters ahead, I will share more of my personal struggles with physical stillness and introduce spiritual truths, exploring the etymology of stillness and related ancient concepts. These insights have guided me in transforming self-defeating thoughts, recognizing self imposed limitations, and creating space for deep healing. They have shown me how to co-create my world in partnership with Spirit, how to welcome grief as a necessary part of life's cycles, and that stillness, ultimately, is an energetic force available to us in every instance we surrender to love.

PART I

An Introduction to Stillness

CHAPTER 1

My Inner Rebel

I used to be one of those people who insisted that meditation was the key to achieving peace of mind. I once believed, as meditation gurus often say, that cultivating inner peace heavily depends on your ability to sit in quiet, still solitude each day. However, after experiencing a dark night of the soul in 2019, my belief in meditation as the sole source of inner stillness began to waver. Today, I view meditation and the pursuit of lasting peace of mind in everyday life very differently. This isn't to say that I no longer see meditation as a powerful practice—through personal experience, I know it to be.

My relationship with meditation began at the age of 11 when my mother introduced us to a spiritual community called Unity that is founded on metaphysical and spiritual truths originating from the New Thought movement. This movement, also referred to as Higher Thought, emerged in the early 19th century and draws on the accumulated wisdom and "ancient thought" from various philosophies and cultures. At the heart of Unity is the belief that divinity exists in every single person, that we are spiritual beings, created in God's image, that the interaction of thought and consciousness within the human mind profoundly impacts our inner and outer worlds, and that spiritual principles alone are not enough - we must live by them. Through members of this spiritual community, I was also introduced to Native American practices, attending drumming circles and my first sweat lodge at the age of 13.

Before discovering Unity and throughout my childhood, I occasionally attended Catholic church with my paternal grandmother. My maternal grandmother, whom I called Momo, introduced me to energy cleansings of Mesoamerican tradition. Both grandmothers shaped my reverence for angels, saints, and Our Lady of Guadalupe, also known as the earth goddess Tonantzin.

Each of these introductions deeply shaped me, leading me throughout my young life to collect works by spiritual leaders, New Thought teachers, healers, shamans, and master philosophers from various eras and cultures. For as long as I can remember, my deepest desire has been to commune with the essence of life and know God in the most profound way. Yet, even with this yearning, I often felt a conflict between the world around me and the truth within me. Despite spiritual exposure, the world I observed as a child and adolescent was marked by anger, disconnection, poverty, and the relentless drive to do more. I also lacked stability as a child and did not feel safe or nurtured by those who raised me, with the exception of my grandmothers.

As a result, I learned to walk a fine line between two realities and as a young, single woman growing into my spiritual practice, I found it possible to realign my connection to God through the practice of meditation. Thus, for a long time, I associated the quality of stillness, peace, and presence with the physical form- void of thought and movement. As I said before, this association began to change when I snapped out of a depressive state in 2019, which had lasted for a year and a half after my youngest son was born.

I consider this instance to be my first awakening moment. By definition, *Awakening* means to experience awareness about a particular event or to wake up, to come into existence, or to become suddenly aware of something. My awakening in Spring of 2019, was that now - as a mother of two, entrepreneur, wife, and trauma survivor, I had somehow adapted to a cycle of running myself ragged. I was living each day just trying to get from point A to point B, so much so that I was leaving my soul's yearning to experience the fullness of life behind. I reached a point in my life of such physical and mental exhaustion, I couldn't see my way out of it.

Not only was I repeating cycles and patterns of my childhood, but I was also passing generational energy of toxic emotions onto my children. This became abundantly clear to me one morning when I saw the fear and stress I had been carrying, reflected back to me through the eyes of my child. Nothing in my life made sense and no amount of meditation could fix it. In fact, meditation became the last thing I wanted to do or felt capable of doing, which surprised me. But nonetheless, I experienced two things:

The first is that meditation felt out of reach and uncomfortable in my body. It was another task I had to add to my already full plate and I judged myself harshly for being incapable of creating that time for myself.

The second is that when moments of meditation were possible, the peace I gained was amazing... and short-lived. Moments later, I'd be at the mercy of the world and losing my shit all over again.

As I became further aware of these experiences, I began to view the practice of meditation very differently than I had before. Then in 2020, I experienced another awakening moment that presented the solution I was looking for, pulling me into a deep understanding of stillness that far exceeded anything I had come across previously. This moment sparked the creation of this book.

On the day of what I consider my second awakening moment, in June of 2020, I was in a downward spiral. I had just received my lowest paycheck as the breadwinner of the family, in the midst of a global pandemic, while also witnessing the fight for basic human decency as people marched in the streets. Like many others, I was deeply concerned about the state of our world and the well-being of my family.

That morning, I woke up as usual, prompted by a small child after little to no sleep, cursing myself for another day lost because I didn't wake early enough to find my center. Anxious dread pulsated through my body; I had no time for presence. I got our children settled with my husband and headed to my office. Then, fueled by toxic stress and caffeine, I proceeded to anxiously make call after call to current and new clients, desperately trying to fix my financial situation with the limited time I had that day.

But, of course, because we are energetic beings, and my energy was nothing less than desperate, no one I spoke to wanted anything to do with me. And who could blame them? Name one desperate, anxious, fearful person you just can't wait to do business with... I'll wait.

After functioning frantically for a couple of hours, all the emotions I was carrying hit me like a ton of bricks. I sat back in my chair, and a familiar feeling arose within me that said, "You're doing too much." My next exhale was like a dam bursting open. I knew it to be true. Once again, I had been swept away by the demands of the world, gripped by the dim appearance of relentless circumstances. No matter what I did, I couldn't seem to catch up. My steps were panic-stricken and directionless, yet I was driven by an overwhelming impulse to keep pushing forward.

I sat back, almost paralyzed, for several minutes before being drawn to the floor. I turned to lie on my back with arms and legs stretched out, grounding myself into the earth. Breath after breath, I let myself sink deeper and deeper. I let emotions and fearful thoughts run rampant in my mind, but this time, I didn't care to stop them. I even embraced them. I wanted to see them.

I can't explain why, but as I lay there, words I had encountered years before, spoken by author and poet Ann Sedwick, entered my mind. She said, "Rebels are those people who refuse the seen, for the unseen."

I found it interesting that of all the words I had read, these were the ones that came to me. I lay on the floor of my office that day for close to two and a half hours. And yes, I know what you're thinking because I thought it too: "Who has two and a half hours to lie on the floor in the middle of a workday?" But aligned with Ann Sedwick's words, this was my *rebel act*. This was me leaning into the unseen abyss of surrender.

Eventually, peace came with clarity. I knew what needed to come next. This time, when I returned to my work, I was grounded in the present moment and released from the fear of outcome. Business goals that I initially assumed would be limited by my 8-hour workday took one hour instead. That week, in the middle of a pandemic, I closed four clients. I was then asked to speak on a national call for the company and 2020 ended up being one of my most prosperous years, financially and otherwise.

Here's where it gets really interesting. Some may be quick to see my time on the floor as a meditation of sorts. One that perhaps encouraged me to return to a daily practice of physical stillness, ultimately leading to my triumphant year. Truth is, there was a time I would have also credited the peace and abundance that opened for me that day to the physical stillness of lying on the floor. I would have woken the next morning with the intention of repeating a similar version of events. I would have recommitted to scheduling this time in my calendar, carrying on the long-held belief that inner peace is only possible when we make time to be physically still. Then, inevitably, I would fail. The dedicated time would go by the wayside, because every day offers a new set of challenges, and there are going to be days when physical stillness is just not possible.

This is important to realize because if one does not find meditation to be an easy or welcomed practice, they will not find peace of mind or do themselves any good in the process. Instead, they will find the practice uncomfortable, and the peace gained will be short-lived once they reenter the hustle of the world.

Late 1900's metaphysical teacher Florence Scovel Shinn called relying on methods of physical stillness "armchair faith". She says, "Armchair faith will never move mountains. In the armchair, in the silence, or meditation, you are filled with the wonder of Truth, and you feel your faith will never waiver... You feel that your God of plenty will wipe out all burdens of debt or limitations. Then you leave your armchair and step out into the arena of life. It's only what you do in the arena that counts."

Since that morning on the floor, my issue with meditation does not concern the practice itself but rather its modern-day portrayal. The common misconceptions include "meditation will solve your problems," "it will become easier and easier with practice," and "10 minutes is all you need for peace of mind - anyone can give that." For someone like me and perhaps for someone like you, the reality is when you are in the depths of despair or flooded with anxiety, 10 minutes is a drop in the ocean.

This time in my life taught me that the practice of physical stillness is simply a vehicle for achieving peace in the moment - it is not the source. And in many ways, it is a vehicle for the privileged. Those who have established material security or the option of solitude that allows them the freedom to enjoy the practice. For instance, those that are single, retired, or empty nesters. As well as those who have experienced a shift in consciousness that leads them to the understanding of the divine right to sit in silence whenever they'd like, or those that were introduced to it at an early age.

I am one of the privileged.

I had the exceptional opportunity of being introduced to meditation at an early age. I also recognize physical stillness to be a divine right meant for any moment. Yet during my dark night of the soul, I finally understood what others meant when they said meditation was not for them. And when I reached my rock bottom, all I knew is that I didn't want stillness only in a single moment I made for myself. I didn't want inner peace with structure and limitations. I wanted it at every moment. I wanted to experience presence and the connection to omnipotence that I know great teachers before us were referring to when they said things like:

"To the mind that is still, the whole universe surrenders." - Laozi

"Stillness is where creativity and solutions are found." - Meister Eckhart

"The stillness in stillness is not the real stillness; only when there is stillness in movement does the universal rhythm manifest." – Bruce Lee

My inner rebel was sparked by the realization that stillness could be much more than a fleeting moment in my day. I became dedicated to uncovering its deeper meaning. Through this commitment, I discovered that the archaic definition of stillness expands beyond our modern interpretation of it as merely a time without movement.

At its essence, stillness is the process of reconnecting with our inherent truth by letting go of societal constructs that influence how we see ourselves and how we engage with the world. It's about embracing our soul's unique path, allowing pain to surface and be replaced by higher thoughts of truth, cultivating the ability to be nonresistant to the natural rhythm of life, the world's conditions, and the personalities around us.

Far beyond the mere absence of movement, stillness embodies a consciousness of peace, presence, and a balanced harmony between awaiting guidance and knowing when to move. A gesture of mind, body, spirit connection that begins in the sacredness of our hearts and has the power to transform the world.

CHAPTER 2

At Some Point in History

Toward the end of my senior year in high school, I was absent a lot because one day I began vomiting every morning and after every meal. At first I kept it a secret. As strange and dangerous as it was, it felt like a burden to admit I was ill and I hoped that what I was experiencing would go away on its own.

Eventually, I told my mother, and she began taking me to various medical professionals. I saw several doctors and specialists, but they all dismissed me as faking, bulimic, or attention seeking. It wasn't until I began vomiting blood and what looked like coffee grounds that anyone took my condition seriously. At my mother's insistence, an ER doctor finally discovered I was hemorrhaging internally due to two bleeding ulcers in my digestive tract. I spent several days in the hospital before returning to life. Within three months, I had lost over 70 pounds. The diagnosis was that the ulcers were caused by a common bacterium, but it was stress that had accelerated the damage.

Stress... accelerated the damage - at the age of seventeen.

Despite being assigned Saturday school to make up for the days I had missed, I skipped my weekend obligation one Saturday to attend a Cherokee sweat lodge.

Early that morning, I sat around the fire with other participants and eventually struck up a conversation with an Elder Cherokee woman. I mentioned to her that I had skipped my weekend obligation to be there because I felt called to the lodge. I wanted ceremony and healing, and I couldn't wait another day. Her response took me by surprise. She said, "At some point in history, we learned to let time tell us when we're hungry. But we don't need time when we learn to listen."

To be honest, in that moment, I didn't fully understand what she meant, but I took it as a nod to my rebellion of skipping school to honor myself. The energy of her words validated my choice to listen to my body, to honor the desire I had for healing, and to choose my wellbeing over external constraints. She delivered a message I desperately needed to hear because my upbringing was one that encouraged conformity and suppressed emotions, but on this day, I was entering the lodge to feel again. I wanted a raw purge of everything I carried inside of me. I wanted freedom.

When this memory resurfaced, as I began writing this book, I spent some time reflecting on my journal entries from that day, gaining a deeper understanding. Today, I see her words as a reminder of all the ways we fail to listen to the longings of our mind, body, and spirit.

"At some point in history," she said, "we learned to let time tell us when we're hungry."

In other words, at some point in life or throughout life, we can become conditioned by our environment to set aside that which brings us joy, presence, and healing for societal constructs that convince us our wellbeing can wait for when the timing is just right.

We might say, "I will care for myself when I have completed my obligations of Saturday school."
"I will enjoy life when I retire."
"I will be present with my children when I'm not busy."
"I will return to peace when I have a moment to sit quietly."

Thereby, we place our unfoldment into little boxes, and we say, "one day I'll get to it".

I believe the path to inner peace, as it is portrayed through images of solitude and quiet - is one of those boxes.

For instance, take a second and consider the idea of stillness for yourself. What does it look like? What imagery comes to mind?

Is it you in a room with lights off, a candle flickering, and eyes closed? Is it someone sitting in solitude, surrounded by perfect weather or with a gorgeous sun setting in the distance? Are you experiencing a moment without your children making their many requests from you? Is it Buddha sitting cross legged beside a slow-moving stream or maybe a canoe floating in calm water?

If so, it wouldn't surprise me. These are the images commonly used to depict stillness. If you were to Google stillness right now, these are the images that will appear and all of which are unlikely scenarios for many lives. My own included, as it has consisted of loss, caring for others, little to no sleep, scary financial situations, and young, active children - on top of working through layers of trauma, that over time, have created barriers, sometimes keeping me from connecting with myself.

Even practices that encourage stillness in motion, such as a walking meditation or yoga, offer their challenges once the session ends. I can recall many times I ran it into the heat of my favorite yoga center, seeking solace on my mat. In that hour, I'd find connection again between my mind, body, and spirit, cultivating inner peace through form and awakening a sense of oneness. Then, shortly after stepping off the mat, an angry email or standstill traffic would throw me off that peaceful edge.

Now, to be clear, I am not dismissing the very powerful benefits physical stillness brings to our mind, body, and spirit. The quiet of solitude and the absence of movement are indeed transformative, especially when the practice flows naturally rather than feeling forced.

However, I also believe there is something to be said about learning to access stillness without needing silence or solitude. It is in those in-between moments that I encourage the practice of tuning into the hunger of your soul first and foremost. This approach is how you learn to ebb and flow with the life you are creating, in such a way that your peace cannot be disturbed by anything outside of yourself, regardless of whether or not you were able to be physically still today.

Beyond my own journey, a significant motivation for writing this book came from hearing workshop participants share their struggles. They spoke of finding peace through physical form challenging, and despite their efforts to cultivate a stillness practice— often influenced by the imagery I mentioned earlier— they found it nearly impossible to maintain consistency or extend that peace into the moments that followed.

One participant said, it wasn't until he retired, after years of depression and anxiety in his career, that he cultivated a practice of physical stillness because he could "finally stop moving". When I reflect on the many different lives we live, the struggles we face, the generational trauma that exists in the mineral of our bones, I hardly think it reasonable to assume peace of mind and presence is only attainable when we stop moving.

I found myself questioning - does it make sense that I criticize my inability to just sit still because that practice is the supposed source of peace? I wonder is it really required that we eliminate movement to experience alignment with a power greater than ourselves, have clarity, or experience longstanding peace of mind? What good are we really to the creation of our destiny or to the world, if that is the case? These questions served as a catalyst for my deep dive into stillness and eventually led me to a definition I had never seen before.

One day on my search, I came across a definition of stillness that defined it as, "a state of freedom from storm or disturbance." A state is a mindset. This definition was referring to stillness as a *mindset*... of freedom... from storm or disturbance.

When I looked further I discovered that the word "stillness", as it is used today, comes from Old English, where it does in fact mean to be motionless, stable, fixed, quiet, calm, and silent. However, in PIE, or Proto-Indo-European, the single tongue that all modern Indo-European languages are derived from, stel-*ni* is the suffixed form of the root *stel* and it is related to establishing order. It means to, "stand, to put in place". Then, in addition to meaning calm and silent, it means to have tranquility, peace, and rest. While the suffix -ness is an element that stands for a quality, a state of being, or a consciousness.

In other words, by this ancient definition, stillness is a state of peace and rest established through order. When I discovered this, I half-expected an angelic symphony to start playing in the background. I began reflecting on all the times I'd felt distress or anxiety, realizing it was always when my thoughts were out of order, fixated on the future or the past, or I was trying to force a favorable outcome that was beyond my control.

Now, think about the moments in your life when you've felt most at peace. What stands out to you about those times?

In my own experience, and through reflections shared by others, I've noticed that peace often comes when we have direction, abundance, or a sense of surrender that lets us release what we can't control. It's when everything feels aligned, moves effortlessly, and we're fully immersed in the present. The common thread in all these moments? A sense of order.

When I discovered this definition of stillness, I thought, what if early references of stillness were not suggesting that we become motionless, but rather that we cultivate a consciousness of peace and rest in-between our movements, as we invite order to manifest.

Not by seeking solitude, but by tuning in to the energy of love we carry within - a force capable of guiding our journey more wisely than anyone or anything outside of ourselves. I have found, in that trust, it is possible to experience inner peace through order, especially in the moments where stillness matters most. When there is no sunset in view or candle to focus on. When the stream is flooding over the bank, the waves are crashing over the canoe, and the children are running wild.

Perhaps it is in these moments that we welcome stillness, as a dynamic state of being, by unapologetically engaging with the natural order of life, finding peaceful rest within the chaos, and remaining rebelliously undisturbed by whatever storm may be present.

CHAPTER 3

The First Law of Heaven

When my oldest son was ten, he shared with me that his biggest fear was getting lost in a crowd and separated from his family. I asked him, "If that were to happen what would you do?" He said he'd probably panic. I told him, if he were ever to experience a scary situation and he didn't know what to do, he must first and foremost do his best to maintain poise and remember that he is never truly alone, so that he can create peace within himself.

I explained that in scary situations, our human reaction is to panic, which is a subconscious mechanism meant to aid in our survival. However, when we panic, we confuse and crowd our minds, producing unhelpful thoughts. We become subject to our environment and vulnerable to what others are doing and saying about us and about our current situation. I assured him that once he establishes peace within himself, whether it be by breathing, walking, or sitting down, he will be able to gain control of his thoughts, observe his situation with clarity, and know what to do next.

It feels counterintuitive for us to maintain poise or stand in peace in a moment of panic. However, without peace, the order of our steps does not come easily, and without order, we become victims of circumstance. In my practice of establishing stillness as a mindset, I've learned that cultivating inner peace and finding rest amid a storm, is connected to my willingness to release the meaning I've attached to my experiences - whether it be the bank account showing negative, a medical diagnosis, being laid off, a pandemic, overwhelming obligations, or getting lost in a crowd.

In today's world, stillness is the act of a rebel because we have been hardwired to believe the cost of wellbeing is to overcome obstacles with force, rather than by inner transformation. This is how history has repeated itself within our own minds.

The human tendency is to believe that the urgency of what is beyond our control holds meaning. As a result, we allow ourselves to be swayed by external forces or past conditioning, becoming fear-driven as we attempt to conquer or sidestep the challenges before us, yet we only deepen our suffering. When we impose our will in this way, we lose touch with our inner wisdom and disconnect from Divine guidance, which is why so many today find themselves unwell—financially, physically, emotionally, and spiritually.

Cultivating a consciousness of stillness takes courage because it requires us to tune into the energy of life rather than lack or limitation. To do this, we must release our ties to the world, regardless of how urgent they may seem, and turn our attention to a Truth that cannot be seen with our physical eyes but felt from within. This doesn't mean we ignore the very real challenges we might be facing at the moment. Quite the opposite actually.   It means embracing the energy of the moment fully and in that pause, finding your place amid the chaos.

The truth is, for every problem there is already a solution waiting. Yet, when panic and fear arise, that is the illusion we cling to, and the consequence is that every anxiety-driven action we take creates a barrier to those solutions. Furthermore, we easily become drifters with no clear idea as to who we are and what we are fully capable of.

When I discovered the early definition of stillness as a mindset of freedom—to allow order through peace and rest—it was in the middle of 2020, and it drastically changed my perspective of the events that were unfolding. This definition gave me permission to transcend the fear that was so pervasive in the world, so that I could focus on my desire for health and inner peace.

One piece of guidance I received encouraged me to stop viewing others as sick. You see, throughout the pandemic, there was so much noise about how invisible COVID-19 was. The media was constantly delivering the message that we or the people around us could be sick without knowing it and that germs could be lingering and lurking anywhere, unseen and undetected. This messaging led me to became more afraid of everyone and everything outside of my household than the possibility of getting sick. Regrettably, I saw every interaction as a potential threat, and it isolated me from others in a way I had never experienced before.

At some point it hit me that this fear was causing separation within myself and in relationship with others. By viewing everyone around me as a potential danger, I was buying into a narrative that promoted disconnection and isolation, despite my desire for community. Realizing this was a turning point for me. It wasn't just about rejecting the fear; it was about tuning into love and reclaiming my ability to share that love with others by viewing them as whole and healthy individuals.

I began to see that maintaining this mindset was an act of rebellion against fear-driven narratives. It was a conscious decision to promote peace within myself by reclaiming my agency over what I could control. Rather than succumbing to widespread panic, I chose to realign with love by intentionally visualizing myself and everyone I encountered that day in perfect health. This gave me peace and as I carried on with my day, I consistently found myself in the right places at the right times, surrounded by the right people. This shift in perspective became an aligned practice that kept me energetically grounded, protected, and attuned to the natural flow of life. As a result, I experienced both abundance and health that year—and in the years that followed.

As the year continued and I sought to further understand the origin of stillness, I began looking at early religious and spiritual texts differently:

"Be Still and Know" – Wait as the order of your steps are revealed, then move forward in peace.

"And Moses answered his people by saying, The Lord will fight for you, you need only to be still." Or the Lord will guide you through every challenge, you need only to rest, as the order of your steps are established – by the Lord, your Inner Knowing, Intuition, The Universe. Whatever name that is for you. The power and grace that comes with this understanding makes much more sense to me because what I know to be true is that we alone are not the source of our good. Our innate goodness is sourced by an omnipotent power working in and through us. To me, these early biblical references of stillness suggest that exact element of co-creative power accessible to all.

In scripture, there is a story of two blind men, appearing in all three gospels of Matthew, Mark, and Luke, which in and of itself connotes significance because not all stories appear in all three gospels. In this story, it is reported that when the blind men called out to Jesus the crowds rebuked them, telling them to "stay in their place". Nevertheless, the blind men continued calling out to Jesus with urgency in their voices. I imagine they were scared they'd miss their opportunity to be healed, and they called out with persistence. Even so, Jesus didn't quicken his pace. He

33

didn't run to their aid; he didn't jump into immediate action. The gospels reveal that Jesus *stood still.*

I personally find it hard to believe this moment was recorded only to announce his physicality. "Well, there's Jesus – he was walking... and now, he's standing still." Considering that he was surrounded by people reaching for him, I'd say physically standing still would only lead to being covered up by the masses. Instead, I believe this was given as an account to his process of inviting order into the space between his movements, allowing him to live his life in alignment with Higher Consciousness.

Jesus, whether you believe him to be part of a story or a real person, was a great teacher of stillness and a master conduit of omnipotence because he understood it was not his works, but the works of a power greater than himself working in and through him. Furthermore, he recognized that stillness was a balance of waiting for order and knowing when to move. A philosophy demonstrated in many parables when he spoke the words, "my time has not yet come."

More than a thousand years before the birth of Christ, this relationship between stillness and action is reflected in the philosophy of Taoism. Laozi, known in modern times as Lao-Tzu, was an ancient Chinese philosopher and author of the legendary Tao Te Ching, which serves as the foundational text of Taoism. Taoism is rooted in the belief that the universe works with order and that we must be able to discern our individual potential through intuitive knowledge. It is said that in his voyages teaching the Tao, Laozi traveled to India and served as a teacher to Siddhartha Gautama, the Buddha.

In the Tao Te Ching, Laozi says, "Action in Harmony with the Tao is called Wu-Wei, literally non-action." The understanding of Wu-Wei is to approach life with acceptance rather than anxious doing or forcing what is out of our control, and without avoiding the problem at hand. Wu-Wei is to wait, and rest, trusting that the solution to any and every problem will come with a readiness to act when action is required.

The balance between movement and stillness is also a fundamental teaching in the interplay of Yin and Yang, a philosophy that regards the coexistence of contradictory forces or elements within the universe. Yin represents cooling, night, form, and *rest*. Yang represents warming, function, day, and *movement*. Deeply rooted in Chinese Philosophy and Taoism, Yin and Yang emphasizes the need for harmony in opposites so that one can have a balanced life.

Chinese philosopher Zhu-Xi explained this further in saying, "When movement reaches its extreme there is stillness and when stillness reaches its extreme, once again there is movement. This alteration of movement and stillness, each serves the root of the other and this is how what is ordained by heaven flows ceaselessly." In other words, when we allow our movements, or action steps, to be balanced by order, we experience heaven on earth. Inner peace, prosperity, health, and the like - regardless of what adversity is swirling outside of ourselves.

In his time, Zhu-Xi shared many reflections that regarded stillness within the context of order. His philosophy, Neo-Confucianism, emerged as an interpretation of Confucian principles, which aspires to cultivate a more rational approach to the metaphysical views of Taoism and Buddhism.

At the heart of Zhu-Xi's teachings lies the conviction that human nature is inherently inclined toward embracing life, and that everyone possesses the potential to attain sagehood, or enlightenment, by embodying the highest virtues. However, he also recognized the influence of external circumstances that distract many of us from this pursuit.

What I find compelling about Zhu-Xi's teaching is his critique of two prevalent notions held by his contemporaries. Firstly, he questioned the effectiveness of achieving sustainable peace of mind through silent meditation. Many philosophers of his time believed that silent meditation could help one return to a peaceful state of being. However, even these philosophers struggled with maintaining inner peace once their meditative sessions ended and external stimuli returned.

Secondly, Zhu-Xi scrutinized the idea of self-regulation and the suppression of problematic emotions, which were also often advocated through meditation or other forms of introspection. He was critical of the notion that merely controlling or suppressing emotions could lead to lasting peace and well-being. Instead, he proposed a different approach. He suggested that by cultivating reverence for the present moment and interconnectedness of all living beings within the cosmos, we could remain attuned to the vitality of life—where our true nature resides — rather than influenced by external stimuli.

This perspective empowers us to face adversity with resilience, letting our interconnected existence guide us in life-affirming ways toward the greater good. By cultivating patience, wisdom, and a sense of harmony, we learn to wait for aligned action, enabling us to serve both ourselves and the world in ways that promote peace.

Even further back, in the earliest records of spirituality and religion, we find the concept of order is deeply embedded in both Indigenous practices and Shamanism. Shamanic traditions involve seeking guidance from the unseen realm, highlighting the connection we have to the spiritual world. Likewise, in many Indigenous practices, existing in stillness is not merely a temporary state but a way of life. Unlike the reasoning logic of Western society, where action is often driven by fear and urgency, these traditions embrace a surrender to the natural order of life. They allow themselves to be guided by the invisible world, which they believe holds a higher wisdom.

In his "Essay on Man", poet Alexander Pope declared that "Order is the first law of Heaven." He says even though it goes against common sense, those that establish order are happier, more rich, wiser, and greater than the rest."

CHAPTER 4

The Space Between Movement

Cultivating a consciousness of stillness in today's world begins by reclaiming your power as a co-creator of your reality. This means boldly embracing your desires, allowing Higher Consciousness to expand and express itself uniquely through you. A common challenge in embracing stillness is that we are all deeply influenced by past conditioning and our environment, which often lead us to rely more on external conditions, or be driven by emotion, rather than guided by our inner wisdom.

Moreover, we've been taught to view grief and burdens as inconvenient—something to bury, push aside, and keep out of the present moment. Yet, when it comes to fostering sustainable inner peace, acknowledging the energy of grief with mindful attention is what welcomes transformation.

This wisdom is demonstrated in the scripture mentioned in the previous chapter. You see, it was not only Jesus that created healing for the blind men. They had a part in their healing as well, which was to follow their desire for sight. This desire was further affirmed by inner wisdom that nudged them forward, even as the crowd rebuked them saying, "Stay in your place!" In other words, the crowd was reminding the blind men of their unworthiness.

The crowd itself could be viewed as a literal crowd or the crowded and self-defeating thoughts of the blind men's minds. Regardless, it is said that *when the moment came for action*, the blind men threw off their cloaks. This act is significant because the cloak symbolized identity. The ragged, dirty, and hole-ridden cloaks represented how the blind men saw themselves. Their inner world, filled with illusions of unworthiness and scarcity, was mirrored by the outer world's rejection. This sentiment echoes the wisdom of many philosophies and psychological insights that suggest our reality is a reflection of our inner world.

This same wisdom teaches that the power we seek for transformation lies not outside ourselves, but always within. Yet, this knowledge often eludes the general public, as seen in descriptions of how the crowds continually flocked to Jesus, imploring him for help. Even as he reminded them, "The works I do, you can do too, and even greater works," they still reached out, pleading to receive what he possessed—unaware that the very power they sought already existed within their own being.

It is also said that when the two blind men cast aside their cloaks, they took the sight of Jesus and continued in *his way*. In other words, they shifted their perception of themselves, embraced their unseen potential, and moved forward in harmony with Christ Consciousness. This act of honoring their inherent value was a rebellious yet ordered step, enabling them to realize the transformative power within, rather than remaining defined by the conditions that bound them. No longer confined by labels and limitations, they unfolded into a renewed sense of self.

In standard English, and true to its etymological origins, the word "unfold" means to spread out or to open something that has been folded, as well as to experience revelation. "Revelation" means to receive communication or knowledge imparted by a Higher Power that leads to a deeper connection with spiritual truth.

Specific to spiritual unfoldment, revelation is to become aware of where we have been disillusioned in life, often reflected in the patterns, thoughts, and habits that no longer serve our highest good. The opening of something that has been folded over is to peel back those layers. Just as it was with the blind men, these layers include identities, illusions of unworthiness, grief from this lifetime, and even energetic ties that have traveled with us from generations before. To unfold is to replace the tattered garments we wear, woven of the past, with seamless cloaks.

Though the opportunity to unfold is always present, I believe for many of us, it takes a life-altering event to bring our attention to the dissatisfaction we feel with our life's conditions, our yearning for a deeper connection, or even the desire to make a difference in the world. It is in these pivotal moments, or through a series of revelations, that the discomfort we feel becomes so intense or prolonged, we finally become willing to embrace another way.

It could be a midlife crisis, parenthood, illness, addiction, or a natural disaster. Regardless of pivot point specifics, it is often during these challenging times that we can sense our soul awaken to that new desire and the opportunity of healing, which is to restore wholeness, to create, or to bring a new experience into being. It is as French author and poet Anais Nin said in her poem *Risk*, "And the day came where the risk it took to remain tight in the bud was more painful than the risk it took to blossom."

A big part in understanding stillness as a state of consciousness is recognizing that healing and creation are intertwined in the pursuit of spiritual unfoldment; they are inseparable aspects of the same process. Each present moment offers an opportunity to transform what we perceive as lacking into awakened potential, which is the inherent strength and power within, waiting to be realized.

Before I understood this, I couldn't stand hearing the phrase, "Just stay in the present moment." I would cringe. I would think to myself, "I'm here, but I wish I wasn't. I have a day full of meetings, a deficient bank account, peanut butter in my hair, and children I'm painfully disconnected with". To me, that phrase was missing depth and direction. How do I stay here? What am I to find within this moment? What happens here?

One weekend, I joined two of my friends for a rare event, a night away at a cabin, and there by a fire, I had a moment of revelation. I was leaning back, looking at the stars, and pondering these questions. I could see the light from the campfire playfully interacting with the night sky and I closed my eyes. I then, in my mind's eye, saw what looked like two conduits of energy running parallel and horizontally from left to right. Eventually, these two conduits came together to form one and I clearly heard, "There is a space between our movements where we have the potential to transform what was into what can be."

What I took these words to mean was that there is a space that exists between our actions—an instance in time, where we can transcend our grievances and create a renewed sense of self, and with it, a new reality. It's not my physicality that dictates my unfoldment, but rather my surrender to harmony and my willingness to act within my sphere of control, guided by love. Sometimes, that next step calls for solitude and silence; other times, it does not.

In our quest for stillness, the best thing we can do for ourselves, is realize that true and sustainable inner peace is not achieved by consuming a spiritual to-do list; it emerges from our willingness to accept our potential - through the guidance of inner knowing, moment by moment, which is a journey as unique as our fingerprints.

There are no set rules or predetermined paths. There is no punishment for missing a meditation, nor is there a need to wait until tomorrow morning or the next yoga session to *be still* again. Stillness is always available, even when we are moving, celebrating, and when we are struck with despair, or triggered by what is out of our control. The present moment is the time for stillness because it is the only time we can establish order within ourselves and align with the rhythm of the universe.

That day in 2020, when I lay on the floor of my office, I didn't just surrender to a moment in the day to be physically still. I threw off my cloak and surrendered to my unseen potential by giving up perceptions regarding how the state of the world was affecting my life and all the ways in which I thought I needed to show up. Instead, I committed myself to the guidance of higher consciousness. Not only did I return to completing my work tasks on that day, but I got really curious about what my journey of unfoldment looked like, and I began to compile what I call The Five Laws of Stillness, which are discussed in this book.

These Laws are a collection of accumulated wisdom from my life and the enlightened knowledge of master teachers throughout history. They served as guideposts to lean into in the spaces between my movements, helping me shift my consciousness from limited perception to one of deep awareness and connection with my inner wisdom—through order.

The 5 Laws are:

The Law of One-Mindedness
The Law of Creating Space
The Law of Co-Creation
The Law of Celebration
The Law of Non-Resistance

What I find fascinating about the order of these laws is that it was not something I consciously planned; they flowed through me in this sequence, and only after completing the outline did I recognize the divine placement of each. For example, we can't fully embrace the Law of Co-Creation without first learning to discern what is ours to do and what is ours to surrender to the universe, as taught by the Law of Creating Space. Similarly, if we acknowledge a power greater than ourselves yet place our faith in worldly conditions and fear-based thoughts—as highlighted by the Law of One-Mindedness—we'll be unable to truly experience the Law of Celebration and the Law of Non-Resistance.

What's beautiful about these laws is that they are not a checklist, nor do they require any specific form. They are simply spiritual truths that foster stillness, guiding us through both times of grief and moments of joy.

Now, before diving into the Laws of Stillness, it's essential to understand why cultivating stillness as a consciousness is so important. There are two reasons:

The first is that we are energetic beings, constantly exchanging energy to one another and with our environment. Our willingness to allow energy to flow and transform within enhances our intuition.

The second reason is that our intuition offers a direct line to universal wisdom and is the foundation for co-creating our reality. As we transform the energy we carry, we release blockages and awaken our creative potential.

I. Energy Matters

When I was a little girl, my maternal grandmother, whom I called Momo, once told me that whenever you find yourself admiring a baby, it's important to offer a slight touch, even if it's just a tap on their little pinky toe or in your mind's eye. Babies are very sensitive to energy, and when they receive too much energy from someone, it can make them inconsolable or even physically ill. Connecting to them is a way of giving a blessing and bridging the flow of that energy. I later learned, this sensitivity is not limited to admiration or to babies; children and adults can also be affected by low vibrational energy, such as being in the presence of an angry or anxious person.

I remember times as a child when I was sick with strange symptoms or inconsolable moods—usually after being around people with angry tendencies—my Momo would perform *limpias* on me, energetic cleanses rooted in Mesoamerican healing practices known as Curanderismo. Curanderismo is a healing art that, like all Indigenous practices, focuses on the mind, spirit, and body connection. These cleanses were a way of clearing out any energy that was not mine and they worked. If you're an empath, or someone who picks up the energy of another easily, you likely already understand this concept of energy transfer.

Life, as a whole, is a network of energy. Each of us, as we live, breathe, and move throughout our day are carrying energy within and transferring that energy to others. Energy is the creative force behind the Big Bang and it is the creation of the world in Christian philosophy. At the center of ancient Shamanic practices and Indigenous healing modalities, energy is recognized as the sacred power inherent in all things. In all matters of life, energy is the driving force of creation.

In the realm of physics, the first law of thermodynamics is the law of conservation of energy. It states that energy within a closed system must remain constant. Energy cannot increase or decrease, but the forms that energy takes are constantly changing. In matters of the universe, this means that the total amount of energy in the world is fixed. We cannot add or subtract energy to the world or ourselves. Regarding matters of life, this is to say that, though energy cannot be created or destroyed, it can be healed and transformed.

The way we carry energy within is through the form of memories, perceptions, and emotions. The most charged form of energy we carry is in our emotions. Our emotions are determined by our perceptions that are influenced by the energy of our past, which we carry as memories and energetic ties from generations before us. When we are born into this world, our emotions are expressed clearly. As babies, we inherently understand how to communicate the energetic charge of emotions we experience, allowing our energy to flow and transform as our needs are met, returning us to a state of rest, peace, and order - our natural state of being.

Over time, our ability to realign with or return to our natural state of being lessens as we are influenced by our external environment, the personalities of those around us, and dependent upon whether our emotional charges are acknowledged, and our needs are met. For many, generationally, they were not and at some point, we learned to resist the flowing nature of energy within. This means that rather than allowing transformation to occur within us, we created barriers and upon reaching adulthood, our reactions to life are often not even connected to the situation at hand, but to the accumulation of preserved energetic perceptions formed by life experiences.

The manifestation of this cycle can be seen on the surface in the patterns of impulsivity and disconnect we act out in life. Whether it be as a result of relationships, financial affairs, sickness, or overall unhappiness, the energy we are holding stagnant within is the root of our troubles. And it is not just the energy of this lifetime but includes the lifetimes of those before us. In many Indigenous cultures, it is said that it takes decades even centuries for the energy of our ancestors to change form. It is believed that everything a person has thought, felt, or endured is recorded in their DNA and passed on to generations that follow. When we are not mindful about the energy we are carrying, we inadvertently pass it on to others, repeat the same detrimental cycles, or easily unravel at life's inconveniences.

I've learned to recognize the energy I carry by becoming aware of my emotional charges and perceptions regarding things like money, raising children, and my marriage. Having experienced poverty, abandonment, and abuse throughout my formative years, I long associated the accumulation of money with working late hours and sacrificing time with those I love most. As a parent, before gaining awareness, I repeated dysfunctional patterns shown to me as a child. In my marriage, I carried an energy of insecurity and was easily offended by the opinions of my husband, which led to a rift in our relationship for a period of time.

Energetic charges are typically referred to as two vibrational frequencies, low and high. Low vibrational frequency is associated with emotions such as anger, fear, anxiety, or guilt. Whereas high vibrational frequency is associated with happiness, joy, and confidence. When low vibrational frequency energy is present, it can cause us to feel stuck, desperate, disordered, and frantic. Not only do these charges create barriers to solutions that will benefit our lives, but when low vibrational energy is frequent and goes unacknowledged, overtime, it manifests in the body as disease. Conversely, high-frequency energy feels free, light, abundant, joyous, and confident. Overtime, high vibrational energy manifests as a strengthened immune system and wide-open channels that allow solutions to appear effortlessly.

As more and more people seek fulfillment in their lives, there has emerged a tendency to label energetic charges as either good or bad. When a low vibrational energy is present, the reaction is often to bypass it by jumping into action, numbing, or resisting. Likewise high-vibrational energy like excitement can lead to impulsive actions aimed at preserving that feeling. On the surface, it may seem beneficial to the ego to react impulsively to these energies or to value one vibration over another. However, this tendency to embrace one frequency while resisting the other perpetuates the illusion that what we feel in the moment is unchanging, dependent on external circumstances, or can be captured somehow. By polarizing emotional charges in this way, we limit the transformative qualities of energy within us. Energy is a force that ebbs and flows. It is natural for it to change frequency in a constantly moving world and that is neither good nor bad. It simply is.

Though it may feel counterintuitive, the key to uncovering order in the present moment is to acknowledge all energetic charges that arise, without labeling them as good or bad, and to release the idea of stillness as something confined to a scheduled time or place. By doing so, you'll find your tolerance for adversity deepens, and the vibrational shift you seek unfolds naturally, without your interference. This inner renewal is then reflected in your outer world and aligned with a more authentic existence.

II. The Gentle Whisper

In the years leading up to my fortieth birthday, many areas of my life seemed to be unraveling, especially my relationships. It's not often spoken about, but when you start to unfold and awaken the creative energy within yourself, you must find new ways of relating to those who are not on the same journey as you. This requires courage to stay true to yourself despite being misunderstood.

For much of my life, especially after having children, I struggled with a sense of belonging. But the gravity of this realization didn't fully sink in until I approached this milestone birthday. I found myself grieving the loss of connection, mourning missed experiences from my youth, and reflecting on mistakes I'd made as a mother. As challenging as it was to embrace these emotions, I knew I had to, to create something different. I felt an inner pull guiding me to release, and often, I'd break down sobbing, surrendering to the intense, low-frequency energy flowing through me with deep acceptance.

There were times it felt as if there was no end to the grief, leading me to question if this was a depression that would never go away or if it would get better over time. However, there was always an inner nudge telling me this was a process of transformation. I had to go through it and eventually, I would be on the other side. I'm glad to say that has been my experience.

What I have learned is that our willingness to honor the energy of the moment, whether it be grief or joy, is directly linked to empowering our intuition. Intuition is the foresight of universal wisdom that resides within every person. It is an inner voice that offers guidance. Sometimes, this guidance is a clear and actionable nudge in the moment. Other times, understanding comes only after the fact, as the message unfolds within us. Either way, trusting your inner voice even when it goes against common sense, is key to staying attuned to spiritual truth.

In scripture, the phrase "still small voice" is used to describe this inner wisdom. The phrase first appears in the story of Elijah in 1 Kings 19 to describe a moment when Elijah experienced God's presence. In its original Hebrew form, the phrase written is קול דממה דקה (qol demamah daqqah) and it translates to "the sound of thin silence" or "a gentle whisper of silence." It represents a moment of transcendent communication, where God's presence is encountered through powerful, yet subtle tranquility rather than audible or forceful sound.

This gentle whisper of silence is where miracles manifest seamlessly, akin to Laozi's notion of "the universe surrenders." It is when we allow space to process emotional charges that the deepest guidance and wisdom emerge, leading us toward healing, creation, and a deeper connection with the spiritual self.

Sometimes, intuition manifests as a feeling in our physical body, often reflected in the phrase, "I felt it in my gut." Other times, it is more of a passing whisper, just as "qol demamah daqqah" describes.

Unfortunately, in our fast-paced world, the practice of trusting the unseen possibilities of inner wisdom is often dismissed, which has caused many to lose sight of their powerful abilities. However, once you choose to become present with your energy, your intuition is given the space to serve you with revelations about yourself and your destiny. First, it reveals layers of erroneous thoughts that need healing, and second, it provides guidance on the next aligned step that is yours to take.

Your intuition, the gentle whisper of silence, communicates in the form of visions, desires, and direction. Visions and desires are connected to purpose, and direction leads to aligned action. We are always being guided and directed, but when we hold energy stagnant, it becomes increasingly difficult to recognize the voice within. The reason it is called the still small voice is because it is a voice of love and love is never forceful or loud. We also exercise free will, which means until we declare willingness to heal and unfold, the spiritual journey is unable to progress.

This is an important lesson because humans are the only beings in the universe, as far as we know of course, with the power to create with their energy and every single person has a gift to share, a life's calling, a desire for themselves and the world they experience. As we have become hardwired with impulsive, anxious doing, it feels natural to dismiss the ideas, visions, and desires that come to our minds and hearts. But, this causes great suffering because life affirming notions are not just trivial fantasies, they are part of our DNA.

I once had the privilege of being included in a panel with three other women in an event discussing toxic emotions. One of the women, who worked with the people of Cherokee, said, "we are living the lives of our ancestors' wildest dreams". That has since stuck with me, as I understand it in connection to other ancestral wisdom that believes just as the energy of our trauma is passed on through generations, so is the energy of ancestral gifts.

Passions and dreams are intrinsic to the nature of your being and whether it be a desire for more loving relationships, better health, to write a book, to sell your art, to spend more time with your children, own a home, have a business, travel the world, the hard truth is these dreams will be with you until your dying day because they are yours to do, which means everything you could possibly need to fulfill these desires has already been provided. You need only say "Yes" and honor the order of your steps.

During the episodes of grief mentioned at the beginning of this section, I was able to recognize and release identities that were holding me back and as a result, I experienced several new beginnings. One of which was an opportunity to work with a friend, Lumbee Elder Black Crow with BIPOC youth. BIPOC stands for Biracial, Indigenous, People of Color. Our work has involved introducing youth from three local organizations to restorative healing practices through nature. It has been a phenomenal and even healing opportunity to be part of a group of medicine people working with children who rarely engage with nature, providing them the space to connect with themselves in the natural world.

Another new beginning was being accepted by another Elder friend Grandmother Redhawk, to intern in the sacred role as both a sweat lodge water pourer and a pipe carrier. One Fall, after attending a Native pipe ceremony, which involves receiving and sending prayers through tobacco smoke, I had a passing thought of myself as a pipe carrier. I didn't think much about it initially, but following this event, on three separate occasions and at times I was mulling over this thought, an eagle flew directly over me. Up until that time, I had never before seen an eagle in the wild.

Eagle medicine symbolizes the power of the Great Spirit and the connection to the Divine, embodying the ability to live in the spiritual realm while staying grounded on Earth. In Native American beliefs, Eagle supports you to have courage and seize opportunities to rise above current limitations. It emphasizes embracing both shadow and light, finding beauty in both, and soaring to new heights. As a totem animal, the eagle embodies the ability to perceive broader truths from a higher perspective, akin to its flight. It is considered the power animal nearest to the Creator. The Eagle also serves as the spirit keeper of the eastern direction in the Native medicine wheel. This is significant to me in my relationship with Curanderismo, where the east is the place of new beginnings, representing the rising sun.

Upon asking Grandmother Redhawk if I could learn from her, I was directed to first send her tobacco to smoke so that she could ask if this was a path meant for me. I am sharing the following with her permission, that after weeks of waiting, I finally heard back from her and her response was that not only was it a "Yes!", but she could see light beneath my feet with every step I took. This information, along with the gentle whisper, were beats on my heart moving me further down a new path.

Before this opportunity presented itself and in private prayer, I used a one-piece Peruvian pipe, but the Native tradition involves using a pipe that is two pieces: a stem and a bowl made of stone that is usually pipestone. Another traditional aspect of becoming a pipe carrier is that the pipe is usually received as a gift, either from an elder or fellow pipe carrier, or through sacred intervention. I had no idea where my pipe would come from.

One evening, I was looking at pipes at various Native American stores online. While I found a couple I considered purchasing, for obvious reasons, it did not feel right to order one online. I also had this inclination to visit a local shop in town. This store sold authentic Native American jewelry and other items of Indigenous origin and was a place I frequented often. Despite not recalling ever seeing a pipe there and finding none listed on their website, I had a persistent knowing that a pipe awaited me.

The next day, I decided to stop by the store. After greeting the owner, I instinctively walked to the back left area of the store. I looked around a stand but did not see a pipe. Instead, I saw a long wooden Native flute, ceremonial talking sticks, sage, and sweetgrass. I reasoned that perhaps I had mistaken the wooden flute for a pipe. The owner, noticing my confusion, asked if she could help me find something. I told her I thought there was a pipe here, but I must have been mistaken.

She informed me that she had pipes on the other side of the store. Upon looking, I realized though they were authentic, they were mostly decorative. I explained that I was looking for one with an L-shaped pipestone bowl for use in ceremonies. After her eyes searched me for a second, she said, "Perhaps I do have something that works for you," and walked to the back left of the store, the exact spot I had been standing by the wooden flute. She reached behind a space in the shelf, and pulled out a bundle of what looked to be old t-shirt scraps.

She unraveled the bundle in front of me, revealing a gorgeous stem adorned with small beads shaped like feathers and a hand-carved pipestone bowl shaped like an eagle's head. As soon as I saw the eagle head, I could feel spirit moving through my body and I immediately shared with her that my initial inclination to do this work was accompanied by three eagle sightings. She listened intently and then suddenly her eyes lit up, and she instructed me to stay still. She pulled out her phone and took a photo of me. She then showed me the photo, revealing that I was standing beneath a large eagle painting hanging in the background, just above where the pipe had been stored.

I was astounded by the experience and grateful to be in the presence of someone who understood the magnitude of the moment. When I asked her how much she wanted for the pipe, she informed me that it had been hidden away for over a year and had never been priced. She was certain it was waiting for me and offered it at a fraction of its worth, both monetarily and sentimentally. This pipe was a gift.

Earlier in this chapter, I mentioned that healing and creation are intertwined in the pursuit of spiritual unfoldment. This means it's essential to trust our inner nudges, even when they defy the logic of the physical world, and to honor the emotional energy of each moment—whether grief, annoyance, or celebration—so we remain open to our potential. The Five Laws of Stillness that follow are designed to help us embrace these energies as they arise in everyday life. On the other side of this practice lies your creative spirit in its fullest expression, rooted in stillness and manifesting as new beginnings.

PART II

The Five Laws of Stillness

The Five Laws of Stillness have profoundly shaped my life, most notably by guiding me to turn toward love in moments of fear and despite external appearances. Through the insights they offer, I have deepened my intuition, embraced my potential, and found it easier to return to inner peace, even amid uncertainty and chaos.

These laws reveal that spiritual unfoldment is not a one-size-fits-all journey but a path of awakening your unique potential through order, guided by the still, small voice of God within. Along this journey, you learn to approach the energy of each moment with reverence and love rather than judgment, transforming your relationship with both past and present conditions. In doing so, you come to experience stillness as a blissful state of being—one that reshapes your reality and leads to an abundant life, grounded in your inherent creativity and worthiness.

May these laws serve you as they have served me.

CHAPTER 5

The Law of One-Mindedness

I choose the path of the highest thought and embrace the unseen realm of omnipotent possibility.

When it comes to spiritual unfoldment, the first lesson is learning how to transcend conditioned thinking, which is the product of accumulated thought energy, not necessarily of your own making, but passed down to you or gained from life experiences. This involves learning to appreciate the mystery inherent in the universe, rather than relying on what the physical eyes perceive as reality. The Law of One-Mindedness is foundational to recognizing stillness as a state of consciousness because it teaches you to become an observer of your thoughts, as well as to unlearn worn-out belief systems and patterns rooted in fear.

This Law addresses our psychology, recognizing that we all carry generational fears and beliefs instilled in us about who we are, what we should be doing, and how we should be doing it. The Law of One-Mindedness creates a foundation to become nonresistant and unbothered by the ever-changing world by welcoming our inner processes. Renewal can then occur as we learn to replace erroneous thoughts — thoughts that keep us stuck—with *the highest thought* rooted in love.

The concept of One-Mindedness first came to my attention through the reference of being "double-minded" as it is stated in the New Testament, specifically in the Book of James. In Greek, "double-minded" is referred to as "Dipsuchos", meaning "two-souled". This term describes a state of internal conflict where individuals are divided in their thoughts, emotions, and intentions.

In original Hebrew, the term is derived from לב לב (lev v'lev), which translates to "heart of a heart". Many biblical scholars, specifically those of ancient Semitic languages, suggest that when "lev" is not being used to refer to the physical organ that pumps blood, then "lev" means "mind". In this context, it means "mind of a mind".

In James 1:5, it says, "If any of you lacks wisdom let him ask of God, who gives to all liberally and without reproach, and it will be given to him. But let him ask in faith, without doubting, for he who doubts is like a wave of the sea driven and tossed by the wind. For let not that man suppose that he will receive anything from the Lord; he is a double-minded man, unstable in all his ways."

This is not to suggest that God punishes those who are unfaithful, but rather highlights the result of believing in two separate worlds: the physical world where outer conditions determine outcomes, and the spiritual world where belief in a Higher Power— God, The Universe, Intuition, or Nature, whatever that is for you—offers boundless solutions.

To be tossed by the wind implies self-inflicted instances of suffering caused by attempting to navigate life through those conflicting perspectives. Though, we may ask for guidance from a Higher Power, for instance, we simultaneously undermine the process by persistently striving to force a favorable outcome, disregarding the solutions available to us through peace, rest, and order.

In pursuit of spiritual unfoldment, to truly progress, you must choose to trust in a Higher Power working in and through you from the soles of your feet to the crown of your head, or just as the waves are driven by the wind, you will be without direction. You will be vulnerable to personalities and conditions that surround you and the belief systems you inherited, rather than your inner knowing.

In psychology, this duality of perspectives is referred to as having a fixed mindset and a growth mindset. Individuals with a fixed mindset tend to be rigid in their views and anchored to past perceptions or inherited identities, limiting their beliefs about who they are and what they can achieve. They tend to view their abilities and intelligence as static, which restricts their potential for growth and change. Conversely, those with a growth mindset focus on the process rather than the outcome. They view challenges as opportunities to learn and grow, emphasizing effort and perseverance. This mindset fosters resilience and adaptability, encouraging individuals to expand their capabilities and embrace new experiences.

In Zen Buddhism, a comparable principle is found in the practice of Shoshin, which advocates for cultivating a beginner's mind rather than a closed one. A beginner's mind is new and unburdened—open, eager, trusting, and free from assumptions. In contrast, a closed mind is characterized by fear of the unknown. Closed-minded individuals find it challenging to embrace a broader perspective because they tend to approach life with preconceived judgments, relying on familiar, outdated ways of thinking. On the other hand, those with a beginner's mind naturally encounter moments of divine goodness, even when fear is present, because they willingly engage with the mysteries of each day.

In spiritual terms, A Course in Miracles references this principle in saying, "You cannot behold the world and know God. Only one is true." Throughout this metaphysical guide, this concept is referred to as separation and union. Separation is to be double-minded in giving power to two narratives. One of which is from your ego and the other is from spirit. Union is to accept the thoughts of the Holy One only, the spirit within, as your own. Thoughts of the Holy

One are the highest of all, seeing no error, no judgment, no guilt, no fear, or lack. Only love.

Even with this understanding, trusting the spiritual world wholeheartedly is easier said than done. We have spent lifetimes being persuaded to conform to loud external voices, rather than surrendering to the quietude of our inner world. Science confirms that, consequently, our brains develop neural pathways from birth that automatically shape our behaviors and beliefs well into adulthood.

The good news is with both ancient wisdom and modern science, we can assist our brains in creating new pathways by understanding its neural plasticity. Neural plasticity is the brain's remarkable ability to change and adapt and is greatly affected by our thoughts. Each thought we have can either strengthen existing neural pathways or create new ones, thus shaping the brain's structure and function over time.

Of course, simply thinking a new thought is not enough. Embracing the concept of "a mind of a mind" encourages you to become an observer. Learning to acknowledge low vibrational energy as a sign of misalignment, and then uncovering the thoughts embedded within that emotional energy, are crucial steps. By countering these thoughts with the highest thought and following up with aligned action—or what I refer to as a *rebel act*—you can, through repetition, create a new belief system and experience transformation.

The Law of One-Mindedness became a significant realization and ordered step for me in October of 2019. That year was one of healing, particularly in my relationships with my children and husband. One evening, I had the privilege of attending an intimate event with Arun Gandhi, Mahatma Gandhi's grandson. Arun shared stories about his grandfather, recounting how, even when he entered Gandhi's study while he was working, he never felt unwelcome. Gandhi never turned him away with phrases I've spoken to my children, like, "Now isn't a good time, I have to get this done," or "I can't play right now, I have too much to do." Instead, Gandhi always welcomed Arun, a gesture that deeply impacted Arun's childhood, especially during his angry years.

Arun's story led me to question some of my interactions with my children, specifically why I believe I can't stop for them when I'm working. Why do I feel their presence is disruptive to the task at hand? My reactive behavior, driven by thoughts of lack, never made sense and always left me feeling regretful. Yet, when faced with continuous stressful deadlines, rigid schedules, accumulating debt, and other adult matters, I found myself defaulting to fixed fears of scarcity rather than the deep love and desire I have to connect with my children. I thought to myself, "If Gandhi had time for children to just wander into his study, so do I."

A few days later, I was hurriedly working on a deadline with only an hour left when my youngest son, Roan, burst into my office to show me his Spiderman costume, the same one he'd been excited about since receiving it months before. When he ran in, every ounce of me was flooded with panic and anxiety, accompanied by thoughts like, "You've got to get this done!" and "There is no time to stop."

I thought of Gandhi and halted everything immediately. I closed my laptop, spun around in my office chair with arms wide open, and pretended I was seeing his costume for the very first time—which, in all honesty, I probably was. On paper, this sounds easy, but the first few minutes were physically painful. I had gotten so used to letting obligations and stress direct my actions that I could feel the attachment to my work task through the anxiety rushing through my body. Every cell felt on edge, but I was determined not to give in.

It wasn't perfect. It's interesting to say this took commitment, surrender, and permission. I had to actually give myself permission to turn toward my son, surrender to the present moment, and commit to the unfoldment of false beliefs that say children can wait. I'd love to say that my thoughts stopped being disruptive instantly, but that wasn't the case. Because my body was so used to anxious doing and putting work first, it entered survival mode. Even through my breath and focused attention on his face, my thoughts were continuing to fire with "what if" scenarios regarding my survival. It was a rebellious act to stand still in that moment rather than give in to the frenetic energy of limited consciousness.

In this space between my movements, I recognized that this feeling of anxious attachment has never been limited to my interactions with my children. It's the same energy that surfaces when the unexpected arises or I'm met with the choice to turn toward something I love and that brings me joy over obligation. The pangs of accepting that shift in present moment attention often leads me to turn away from these life-fulfilling gestures, giving in instead to the weight of societal expectations.

This is why I believe Jesus stood still all those times. He wasn't merely becoming motionless; he was waiting for order, which always begins in our thoughts. In those moments, he stood still to transcend his human consciousness, by remembering that *it was not his works,* but that he was a channel of omnipotence. This surrender enabled him to lovingly and rebelliously redirect his attention to take his ordered step in the moment, which was especially important when it defied societal norms.

After only a few minutes, my son went on his way, and I sat back relieved to see that I had survived the moment, before proceeding to complete my deadline with ease and a clear head. What I know to be true is that entering my son's world in that exact moment was to *be still* because embracing his presence was an ordered step. Despite the conflicting thoughts surfacing, I resolved to align with the path of highest thought—choosing instead to believe that my son is a manifestation of love. *Anything born of love cannot deplete me of time, money, or any other resource.*

Through the repetition of this new focused belief, I can say today that it has reshaped my reality. When I turn toward my children, even at the busiest of times, I never miss an opportunity for abundance or run out of time to complete a business task. This is a neural pathway I created. However, at the time this story took place, it truly was an act of defiance for me to prioritize my son over my workload and the anxiety coursing through my body. Through my commitment, however, I not only showed him love but also began to heal a generational narrative embedded in my DNA— that says, "work comes first" and "children are better seen than heard." The latter being a Victorian-era notion that implies that children should be obedient, quiet, and adaptable to adult needs.

This ideology was taught to me as a child, where I was not well nurtured and there was no space for me to express myself. After I had my second child, this belief was represented in a magnet I received from an older relative that said, "You spend the first two years helping your child speak and walk and the next sixteen telling them to sit down and shut up."

In the early stages of motherhood, I found myself channeling that same energy with my children—not intentionally, but as a nagging habit that clung to me. I struggled to turn toward them when pressed for time and to create space for their individuality to unfold. This tendency wasn't born from my own desire; it was an inherited habit passed down through my Mexican lineage, a survival mechanism rooted in a history of cultural loss. Once I realized that my deep desire was to break away from this ingrained pattern, I began to see how I had been living in a double-minded way: prioritizing the urgency of the world while simultaneously trying to experience the love of God, as it is channeled through my children and other fulfilling opportunities that arise.

Instead of recognizing my children as conduits of love and prosperity meant to be embraced presently, even the moments I perceived to be inconvenient, I thought of them as bodies to be managed. It is important to acknowledge the spiritual harm children endure when they are fed directives on what to think, how to be, and when it is the appropriate time for them - all of which are closed minded ideologies shaped by generational energies that have never served our highest good. This is how double-mindedness is inherited and perpetuated. The influences of our past and external circumstances tempt us to forsake our spiritual self that senses the Truth in these outlooks to conform.

When we become aware of this, as adults, it becomes our sacred duty to transform every thought and action not aligned with love, to counter these influences.

In 2020, it became somewhat normalized to have children running around in the background and my ability to integrate my children was positively influenced that year. An image I'll never forget was a male news reporter mid interview, in his home office, when his children came waddling in followed by his wife, busting through the door to stop them. It was interesting to witness the reporter shoo away his toddler as if we couldn't see her there.

I couldn't help but think how beautiful it would have been to see this man embrace his children calmly on-air allowing time for his wife to come and gently take them away. Which of those images transfers a sense of peace to you? The second, right? Because that image is stillness in action. His children were part of his present moment experience. Turning toward them was his ordered step and nothing but good could have come from embracing that moment with them. Just think of the publicity.

In learning how to create a new neural pathway and align with one-mindedness when it comes to my children, I've received wonderful encouragement from my friend Black Crow, an Elder of the Lumbee tribe. Whether I'm attending events or helping her facilitate ceremonies, she always asks me to bring my children. "That is the Native way. Children are supposed to be here with us.", she would say, and I would think, but isn't this a "sacred prayer ceremony?" How can we pray and experience stillness with loud, excited voices in the background?

Looking back, it seems almost absurd to have questioned it. How could the sacredness of that experience, or any for that matter, be disrupted by the love and connection to the Divine all children bring to this Earth? My minister friend, Reverend Darlene expressed the same insight. She said, "Don't ever worry about bringing your baby into the service. If he "disrupts" someone's meditation, it means that person is missing the point." How right she is and once again this speaks to my position that meditation is purely a vehicle for stillness, it is not the source.

Other instances of double-minded thinking can happen in business affairs, when money is tight, or in any instance of anxiety. In business, perhaps there are feelings of regret about making a decision. The thought behind this is likely that this mistake will cost you or that you're not good enough, or smart enough. One-mindedness would be to turn your attention to a new belief such as, "Every decision I make is a valuable lesson that contributes to my growth and success. I trust that even mistakes lead to new opportunities and insights."

When money feels tight and bills are looming, a split mind is having faith in a Higher Power while exhausting oneself trying to figure out how to force a favorable outcome. Realigning to one-mindedness could be to believe, "I trust that abundance flows to me effortlessly and that I am supported by a power greater than myself. I release the need to control and I allow solutions to come naturally."

In instances of anxiety, perhaps from feeling like you've said something wrong or worrying about what others think of you, realigning with one-mindedness could be saying to yourself, "Regardless of my mistakes, I choose to be at peace with who I am. May any and all errors I've made now be transformed to serve my highest good and the highest good of all others, as I release the need for approval and embrace my unique path."

A source of inner peace comes when you train your thoughts to align with God Mind or *the highest thought*. Once again, this doesn't necessarily come easy because of a lifetime giving way to anxious and fearful thinking. Therefore, it requires anchoring into truths that were not taught, but that you learn to accept at the core of your being as Truth. Such as the following that I call Mantras of The Highest Thought, but better yet, rewritten in your own words:

I have unique gifts inside of me, waiting to be expressed.

Universal abundance is the source of my good and nothing outside of myself can ever take from me what is mine by divine right.

Even when I make a mistake, I trust that I am always supported and there is a solution within reach.

When I nurture what is mine to nurture, such as my body with self-care, my children with loving affection, and my emotional wellbeing, the universe nurtures me.

Even as external situations look and feel scary, everything is falling into place as it should because I am worthy and supported by God, The Great Creator, the Universe, the Cosmos, Pachamama (- whatever that omnipotent power is for you).

There is nowhere I AM, that God is not.

The Law of One-Mindedness provides the opportunity to liberate oneself from false belief systems by actively choosing thoughts that align with the highest thought. This understanding makes this Law the foundational piece for the remaining Laws because it focuses on reshaping ingrained thought patterns. It's essential to understand that merely speaking positive words isn't sufficient, and resisting negative or low vibrational thoughts is counterproductive because thoughts are energy, immutable in their vibrational nature. Therefore, our approach must emphasize transformation, where aligned action follows aligned thoughts. In the case of rewiring belief systems, the aligned action is repetition.

When anxiety or fear creeps in, the rebel act is to observe our emotional state to find the limited thought that fear is linked to and create a new default neural pathway by choosing to believe the opposite is true.

If you're uncertain about which faulty systems influence you, your energetic charges always act as your internal compass. Low vibrational frequencies like fear and anxiety indicate areas needing alignment or healing. Rather than resisting, your role is to allow the emotional energy to be acknowledged, then affirm the highest thought with repetition until peace takes the place of fear. Do nothing else but this, and on the other side of fear, you will receive solutions, packaged in love and delivered by the gentle whisper of your soul, wherever you may find yourself.

CHAPTER 6

The Law of Creating Space

As I let go of what no longer serves me, I create space within to realize my expanded potential and welcome infinite abundance in every aspect of my life.

At the very center of your being exists a bright luminous light. This light represents your truest expression of self. The part of you that is fully connected to a source that cannot be seen with your physical eyes. This light was brightest when you were born.

However, as you grew into this world, like everyone else, you were taught how to think, who to be, what to do, and what you were capable of by society and the personalities that raised you. You may have even lived through traumatic events that covered your light little by little or in one swift burial. These experiences added protective layers, concealing your light and influencing you to unlearn the connection you have to the inner voice of wisdom, which serves as your bridge to the unseen realm.

At some point in life, it may become abundantly clear that you must peel back those layers and uncover the greatness that is *your* light. This is where stillness is more deeply discovered through the Law of Creating Space, which acknowledges that every advancement in life requires the release of something old. In other words, to bring something new into your life, you must let go of what no longer serves you. This Law goes hand in hand with The Law of One-Mindedness because transforming your belief system is further advanced through the aligned action of mindful release.

Overall, it is important to practice releasing because we tend to stay filled up. Holding close everything from grief, worries, memories, to physical items we've acquired over time. In these ways, we have become accustomed to bringing in and rarely letting go. Overtime, various life factors accumulate, eventually manifesting in the physical body. I experienced this during my dark night of the soul when I had taken on a variety of obligations that left me unfulfilled. I was absolutely consumed with the noise of my environment. What started as anxiety that became more and more frequent eventually turned into physical illness and I found myself incapable of mindfulness or acclimating to energetic freedom.

The Law of One-Mindedness helped me to redirect my thoughts when fear was present. Then the Law of Creating Space showed me what I was being called to release. What I realized as I began practicing the Law of One-Mindedness through Mantras of The Highest Thought and rebel acts is that on the other side of realignment, is revelation. Revelation is the art of receiving messages from Higher Consciousness. The actual definition of revelation comes from the 13th century and is described as the disclosure of information by a divine agency; to unveil; to uncover.

The truth is, we are always being given messages through ideas, images, and memories. However, because we are so consumed by mental chatter, we fail to acknowledge these insights or we consider them to be idle thoughts. This is a mistake because these messages hold answers regarding the layers we carry that separate us from love. The great mystic and Sufi poet Rumi wrote, "Your task is not to seek for love, but merely to seek and find all the barriers within yourself that you have built against it."

The Law of Creating Space comes after The Law of One- Mindedness because messages of the Holy One are quiet like whispers. It is an aligned action to make room for those whispers to be mindfully received. Throughout my experience, the messages I receive are gentle flutters that drift through my consciousness. Sometimes, it's a persistent nudge to organize a cluttered closet, a seemingly random memory, or a mental image of someone I've lost touch with. Each whisper provides an opportunity to reclaim conscious connection to the barrier I've built and the layer I'm being guided to unfold.

Most of the time the revelation I receive comes in the form of memories and insights that are directly related to what had triggered the dis-ease I had been feeling moments prior. I've learned that in every present moment, we have the propensity to unintentionally bring our past with us whether it be by attaching to physical items, circulating harmful thoughts, or holding grudges. We tend to behave as though the past is no longer the present, but our past exists in our patterns. Revelation is how we come to recognize the past that lives between the words we speak, the thoughts we think, and the way in which we connect with ourselves and one another.

The Law of Creating Space is a practice of allowing the past to come to the surface. It is about owning everything about yourself and coming into alignment with what you may perceive as the good, the bad, and the ugly. This is another rebellious act against societal demands that have coerced us into believing inconvenient aspects of self must stay hidden. This belief fails to realize that aspects of self are never truly hidden because our pain is not just our own. We share it with one another through our disconnect, judgment, and inability to walk in loving presence with those unlike us. What we must learn is that freedom is found when the past is brought to the surface and in taking this journey ourselves, we can empower others to do the same.

One of the most profound experiences of revelation I've ever had, helped me to uncover one of the greatest barriers I had to love. The information I received didn't come to me in one swift arrival, but over a series of weeks where I kept catching a glimpse of an event that occurred when I was nineteen. It was the same each time. Me and my friend, arriving at a party. We were at the trunk of her car, grabbing liquor, before she slammed the hood down on my left fingers. We laughed about it. I remember the throbbing pain and thinking, "At least I'm too drunk to really feel this." For weeks, this was all I was given. I didn't remember anything outside of this scene.

The significance in this, is that at the time this memory was returning to me, April of 2020, I was in a lot of pain, and I was asking for freedom. I was asking for guidance, love, presence, healing, affluence, and so much more. I didn't think the two instances were related, but what I soon learned was that this memory was the source of a false narrative that I needed to heal. Over the course of a few weeks, the memory became more and more frequent. It fluttered through my mind when I was doing laundry, driving, walking. The same clip would replay in my thoughts. Eventually, I began to ask, "What does this mean? What do I need to know about myself?"

One day, I was standing at my kitchen counter preparing lunch for my family, as they were happily playing outside together, and the vault opened. Not only did the memory in its entirety emerge, but I could see clearly all the barriers I had built to hide behind. I was guided to write every painful detail down and with each stroke of my pen, I could see how this piece of my past had traveled with me and woven itself into life events that followed. Without my even knowing it, I carried the burdens of shame and anger around with me like an old friend. As I brought this story to the surface, I allowed myself to grieve what had happened, and over time, I was able to cultivate grace, love, and compassion for myself. What came next was a sense of permission to lay down this burden of what I had been through and pull away the layer placed upon my luminous light.

Sometimes, we are frightened at the thought of bringing past realities to the surface, but what must be understood is that this is not about forcing a deep dive into your past, but rather being available to intuitive whispers that reveal exactly what you need to know, when you need to know it. In each instance I have received an insight of my past, I have also been shown the immense power of love the universe holds for us. Every single time, regardless of what the memory is, it is delivered to me in such a way that I am not overcome by the unveiling. I can look at the event knowing that there is always a new beginning if I am willing to *be still* in all matters of life.

The Law of Creating Space is a lesson of releasing energetic ties to our past and it is also a lesson of circulation, as in giving and receiving. As you learn to give of yourself, releasing what no longer serves you, you are creating space for the Holy Spirit to give to you. There are three areas in life we can experience the gifts of stillness by creating space: physically, mentally, and spiritually.

Create Space Physically

On the physical level, the easiest way to create space is to let go of items in your life that you no longer need, want, or use. This is how you create what many spiritual teachers refer to as a vacuum, which comes from a physics concept attributed to Aristotle called horror vacui in its original Latin. The basic principle states that "nature abhors a vacuum". Meaning that in the natural world, empty spaces are nonexistent because there is always something available to fill the void. When something is removed, it will always and immediately be replaced by something else. Most people today are congested in some way, whether it be with physical items, thoughts, or grudges. The first way to create space is to give up what you no longer need on the physical level.

I learned this practice early in life and it has stayed with me because it does not fail. Every time I create space in my physical environment I experience abundance, usually in the form of financial gifts. When I'm feeling stuck in place, desire to have opportunities, or have failed to receive money I'm expecting, the first questions I ask are, "What needs to go? Where do I need order? Where do I need space?" I then get to work decluttering my office, a drawer, my closet. Anything that has accumulated clutter. Many times, those areas that I clear out are ones that I've held in the back of my mind or on a to do list for a while. A reflection of the tendency to dismiss intuitive whispers meant for my greatest good.

In July of 2020, in the middle of the pandemic, my paycheck was much smaller than it had ever been, and my husband had just been laid off. On the surface, it seemed as though we should keep a watchful eye on our finances and not make any "unnecessary" purchases. The first week of June, however, I began getting this nudge that our garage, which had been filled to the max for several months, needed to be cleaned out. The garage had become a catch all of sorts with large items that were broken, along with items we didn't need or use any longer. To successfully clear everything out, we would need to rent a dumpster that would cost a few hundred dollars and of course, have time to complete the task.

As this was lingering in the back of my mind, I was doing everything I could to keep my business running, but I felt like I was getting nowhere. As the days progressed, the idea of clearing out the garage became more and more persistent, even with my attempts to shoo it away because of both the time it would take and how costly it would be, especially when my reasoning eye was on the number in our bank account and the amount of work hours I thought I *needed* to put in. Finally, one day, I became aware of how insistent this idea had become and I remembered this universal Law of creating space. I called the dumpster service, despite my fear of lack, and in one day, my husband and I sorted what could be salvaged for our local thrift stores, recycled as much as we could, and tossed everything else.

The very next day, I received a draft into my account from a client that was months past due. Two days later, my husband received an unexpected check from his work.

Another example comes as I am writing this chapter, November 2023. For several weeks I had felt stagnant with my writing. I had also applied for a grant in September, but had not yet heard back, so I assumed I was not a recipient. At the same time, my office was in such disarray that I had moved to my kitchen table to complete my work each day. Over days, this sense of frustration and confinement began to intensify. I woke up one day and knew I had to get my office in order.

Again, I sorted, donated, recycled, and tossed out everything I no longer used. When all was completed, not only did I give myself immediate freedom on the physical level, but I also opened the space for abundance. Words began to flow through me again and two days later, I received a call from a woman with the grant organization I was waiting to hear back from. She said they had been trying to reach me, but for some reason their emails were blocked from getting to me. It turned out, my grant proposal had been accepted.

Then three days later, I was approached by a friend I had worked with on an event three months prior. She said I did such good work that the sponsoring organization wanted to give me additional money.

It may sound unbelievable, but if you allow yourself to consider this idea, the reciprocity makes perfect sense to the self-organizing universe of which we play a part. The rule of nature is to flow the energy of creation – money, opportunity, talent, health is all a manifestation of that. When space is created in our natural world, evolution of some kind takes place to fill that void and create balance. The same principle exists for us. When our physical world is overwhelmed with clutter, we have an opportunity to create space for universal abundance by clearing out the mess.

In addition to clearing out spaces in our environment, creating space also includes caring for the body with physical activity as well as eating as many foods that are touched by the sun, as in real food versus processed, which not only benefits our physical well-being but also aligns us more closely with the natural rhythms and energies of the earth.

Another way to create space is by giving to others and viewing money as a tool that is meant for circulation. It is no secret that giving, when it is an aligned action done without condition, is among the best ways to increase our happiness. Many studies have been conducted suggesting as much. Giving away items or gifts, a listening ear, and support when energy is mutually aligned are all ways we create space within. As such, we become vessels of affluence, which means to flow abundantly, according to the etymological definition. Just as creation flows freely in nature, so does abundance flow through us if we allow space for it.

Regarding money, The Law of Creating Space aims to adjust the conditioning that sees money as something to hoard and save. Money is a tool, and it is meant to circulate and be used as such. Many people take on attitudes about money that contradict the way in which they operate in day-to-day life. Such as saying that money doesn't matter, but then working every day of their lives to get it. Another inherited belief is that money is the root of evil, or that it is bad to have money. The truth is money does matter because it is matter formed by the energy of thought. In this human experience, money is what allows us the ability to promote wellbeing for ourselves and others. Therefore, it is a divine resource.

The best way to circulate money is through the practice of tithing. Many people have a distaste and a misunderstanding about the concept of tithing, usually due to religious organizations that insist members give out of obligation, rather than treating it as a sacred practice that acknowledges the relationship between the individual and the infinite source of all supply. Today, tithing is mostly recognized as a gift of the first tenth of all income to whomever or wherever you receive spiritual food.

The word "tithe" has its origins in Hebrew. It comes from the Hebrew word מַעֲשֵׂר (ma'aser) which means "a tenth part." In ancient Hebrew culture, tithing referred to the practice of giving one-tenth of one's income or produce as an offering, typically for religious or communal purposes. In my experience, I've found that there is a certain kind of magic that happens in my mind when I give financially through a Tithe, as it serves as a routine way of releasing the meaning I attach to money.

I believe this is because tithing, at its core, is an energetic exchange that demonstrates faith in universal substance, which promises to always fill the void. The practice of tithing is one of systematic giving, rather than improvised giving that occurs when approached by a nonprofit or person in need, for example. Giving to charity and those in need is of course a noble deed but is not to be confused with or take the place of returning a portion of what you have earned back to the universe, the true source of your supply.

I learned to tithe at an early age, when I was introduced to spirituality, and it has since been a routine that continues to bring forth a great deal of prosperity in my life. When I receive income, before I pay bills, I give a tenth to whomever has blessed my spirit. I've given to Shamans, elders, churches, spiritual workshop facilitators, a server who blessed me with insight, teachers, etc. When I give, it is an intimate and personal choice of love and gratitude for those who share their light with me. I've tithed when the income I received has looked like not enough and I've tithed when the income I received was the highest it's ever been. From this, I learned long ago that the amount of income I receive has never made a difference to the thought I have that says I need to keep all of it for myself - just in case. Tithing is my rebel act to thoughts of scarcity that consider money to be a limited resource. I give, despite the fear, as a declaration that I will not be held captive by money. I will not be coerced into believing my good is limited. I will instead allow money to be a tool for creating further abundance. As a result, I consistently observe that when I give systematically, the universe reciprocates systematically.

Writer Ralph Waldo Emerson unraveled this principle in his essay "Compensation", where he reflected upon the idea that there is reciprocity in life that promises we will always receive what we give. He claims the universe operates this way because it requires balance and is harmonious in all its workings.

This Law also applies to giving to all those who are owed, including bill collectors. Many people have an immediate sensation of doom when a bill comes in the mail. The ultimate combatant for this, is to pay it with total and complete love in your heart and mind. To look at each bill as if it is a friend, rather than a threat and see it as an opportunity to circulate abundance. Remembering The Law of One-Mindedness can help as you anchor into the Truth that you are always supported and voids of any kind will always be filled at the right and perfect time.

An understanding I am fond of can be found in the sacred way of First Nations people where giving is a central part of the culture that represents gratitude, honor, and maintains the harmony needed to hold the community together. More importantly, the culture of giving and receiving is not like that of today's major society where the giver is noticed for generosity. Instead, giving is an act of prayer and a reminder of the spiritual force that underlies all of existence.

Practice The Physical Law of Creating Space:

1. Clean out cluttered spaces.
2. Give away anything you no longer use or want.
3. Tithe a tenth of all you receive for six months, even if fear is present, and record the increase in financial substance and opportunities that you experience as a reminder to continue this spiritual Law. As it states in Malachi 3:10, "Bring the whole tithe into the storehouse, that there may be food in my house. "Test me in this," says the Lord Almighty (or Universe, Holy Spirit, Great Creator), "and see if I will not throw open the floodgates of heaven and pour out so much blessing that there will not be room enough to store it."
4. Be friendly with bills.

Create Space Mentally

Just as physical clutter in our surroundings can block the effortless flow of universal supply, so too can mental clutter. While identifying and addressing physical clutter is often straightforward, recognizing the mental clutter that occupies our minds requires a deeper level of awareness, especially since most of our thoughts are the same thoughts as the day before. In fact, neuroscientists and psychologists suggest that 95% of our thoughts in this moment are the same as those we had yesterday. Much of this has to do with the influence of our subconscious mind, which is the collective consciousness of our default neural pathways.

For the most part, the subconscious mind has garnered a negative reputation due to its tendency to loop self-sabotaging thoughts. However, it can also serve as a valuable ally. As observers of our thoughts, we may discover that the subconscious mind excels at highlighting unresolved issues or lingering concerns that require our attention.

Historically, before the pervasive influence of media and technology, our lives were more intertwined with the natural world, fostering a balanced relationship with the subconscious mind. When unresolved issues accumulated in our subconscious, generations before us recognized emotional charges as signals to prioritize rest. They embraced deep sleep and welcomed moments of idleness and boredom through activities like connecting with nature, walking, and simply sitting in contemplation. These practices helped maintain clarity in their subconscious minds and ensured the free flow of energy.

However, today's fast-paced lifestyles have reshaped our approach to restful moments, replacing them with a constant quest for mental stimulation. Our minds are inundated with stimuli—from worrying on the go, to accumulating possessions, to endless scrolling. Despite our belief in mastering multitasking, it's really our subconscious mind that functions as an all-encompassing filing cabinet, noting unresolved matters and adding them to an ever-expanding backlog.

The repercussion of this is a cluttered mental space, which then manifests as anxiety, overwhelm, stress, diminished motivation, difficulty concentrating, and sleep disturbances. When these symptoms persist in daily life, this indicates an overworked subconscious mind. Dreams, emotions, and spontaneous thoughts are all symptomatic of a cluttered cognition, indicating that our subconscious is filled to the brim, and we no longer have room to create.

Clearing the clutter of the mind requires commitment to establish external and internal boundaries. External boundaries mean considering what content you are allowing your mind to take in and redirecting as necessary. It means consciously limiting mental stimulation like screen time or frantic activity by acclimating to moments of decompression and connection. Internally, setting boundaries is to exercise conscious control over your thoughts, deciding when matters are not fit for contemplation, guiding your mind to defer worries for another time, and asking for revelation about your emotional charges.

When I was lying on the floor of my office in 2020, another key factor in my attainment of peace that day was choosing to unravel my subconscious mind by embracing what it wanted me to resolve. Instead of seeking to quiet the paralyzing energy I held, I began discerning its roots first through The Law of One-Mindedness, so that I could then know what to release.

The scarcity fueled thoughts firing in my brain were:
What about the bills due next week?
I'm not spending enough time with my boys.
I'll never make this business work, especially through a pandemic.

Money is limited.

These worrisome thoughts act like anchors lodged beneath the seabed. Despite my earnest desire to sail freely, pushing my ship forward only causes the anchors to snag and impede my progress. However, by allowing my awareness to hover directly above each anchor, acknowledging its presence, I can pull it to the surface. In doing so, I find the freedom to move forward.

Likewise, once you become aware of the mental clutter keeping you anchored, a helpful approach to acknowledge unresolved issues is to participate in a morning brain dump by writing down everything on your mind during moments of overwhelm—tasks to complete, worries, fears, fleeting memories, regrets, and even what you feel grateful for or wish to celebrate.

Once you're aware of what occupies your mental space, when your subconscious mind attempts to remind you of an unresolved issue later in the day, you can address each concern as if advising a friend. For example, when a worry resurfaces, you might say to yourself, "Now isn't the time for this concern. I recognize this bill is due in two days. If a solution isn't found by 10 am tomorrow, I'll worry about it then," or "This isn't the right moment for worry, but I will make the time to bond with my children at 3 p.m. today."

This technique may seem simple or too good to be true, yet it has worked really well for me, coaching clients, and workshop participants. By offering the subconscious mind resolution when those worries arise, I've discovered that my anxious emotional state

lessons and solutions naturally emerge within the
timeframe I've consciously set. Such as, I sign an
unexpected client at the last possible second or my
children approach me with the perfect idea for us to
bond.

There are also times when emotional charges arise
out of the blue and I find it difficult to pinpoint the
root thought behind them. In these moments, I find
resolve by asking myself what I call *soul questions*.
Often we ask the question "why me?" and then
wonder why we don't get an answer or why things
don't change. The reason is "why me?" isn't really a
question that gives space for an answer. The response
of Infinite Intelligence will always be, "Why not you?
Are you not a channel of omnipotent solutions?"

Soul questions help us transform mental clutter
because they are asked with the intention of
discovering the history of related energetic charges,
and they encourage continued connection with inner
wisdom. Soul questions are life-affirming such as:
What do I need to know about myself?
What is this experience teaching me?
*How can I see this as Infinite God Mind and Universal
love would see this?*
What scares me about this situation?

Because the subconscious mind is deeply influenced
by imagery, the guidance that comes from asking soul
questions often appears in the form of memories that
reveal what initially triggered the fear in the first
place.

When I began writing this book, I encountered fear
and doubt consistently, but for the most part I was

able to resolve what came up with the tools I mentioned above. However, one evening, I was sitting on my couch, working on the outline for this book, and a wave of dread engulfed me seemingly out of nowhere. I started sweating, breathing heavily, feeling tense. Every part of my body seemed to be screaming, "What are you doing? This doesn't make sense. Who's going to listen to you? Who's going to even care?" I was paralyzed. Closing my laptop, I took a deep breath and desperately vocalized, "What is this? Why do I feel this way?"

Almost instantly, in my mind's eye, I was transported back to the summer I turned twelve, the same year I discovered spirituality. I was in Texas, visiting my dad, who had given me a bright pink Huffy bike for my birthday. One day, while he was at work, I had the idea to write notes of oneness, abundance, and love, before delivering them to people's mailboxes. When my dad came home that evening and asked me about it, having heard a neighbor mention a girl on a bright pink bike placing notes in mailboxes, I denied it was me.

As innocent and wholehearted as my actions were, I remember feeling like I had outed myself. In those days, my environment, which was predominantly Catholic, didn't provide room to express my unique self and I didn't feel safe being me. Outside of toxic and angry environments, another factor was that I didn't have very much stability. I was shuttled back and forth from state-to-state multiple times a year as I traveled from Alabama or Tennessee to Texas, staying with various family members, friends and some random people. I found it difficult to cultivate a sense of belonging. So much so, that consequently, I learned to suppress my desires and expressions, attempting to fit in.

Recognizing the connection between writing this book and the fear that engulfed me from that day on my pink bike was a pivotal moment. It revealed how deeply ingrained fears from my formative years were interfering with my current desire. Venturing into a new direction triggered my subconscious mind's instinct to keep me safe by keeping me small. My body re-experienced sensations linked to my youth—fear, shame of being different, regret, and a yearning for acceptance. This revelation guided me to identify and confront the energetic charges that were holding me back.

When actively engaging in the process of creating mental space, we confront the duality of our thoughts. In this instance, I carried within me the content of this book, a deep desire to connect spiritually with others, and a dream placed on my heart. However, my mind was also cluttered with past conditioning that urged me to remain stagnant for safety's sake. Bringing this awareness to light allowed me to utilize both the Law of Creating Space and the Law of One-Mindedness by realigning with a mantra of the highest thought:

I am choosing to release that moment in time that no longer serves me and I am now free to embrace my desires.

The significance of clearing out a cluttered mind resonates in Hawaiian culture, where the image of an empty bowl holds symbolic meaning. An empty bowl represents potential and promise, serving as a vessel for holding light. Bowl making is even considered a sacred practice, emphasizing the importance of releasing worn out thoughts until our vessels are emptied, so that light can continue its effortless flow. Throughout our lives, outdated beliefs and to-do lists can accumulate in our metaphorical bowls. It is our responsibility to clear them out daily, ensuring that our vessels remain open and ready to receive new insights and experiences.

Practice the Mental Law of Creating Space:

1. Recognize low frequency energetic charges such as anxiety, overwhelm, decreased motivation, stress, etc. as cues letting you know something is unresolved in your subconscious.
2. Defer the worry for another time or ask a life affirming question related to the moment: What is this feeling about? What do I need to know about myself?
3. Empty your mental bowl by releasing everything in your mind onto paper and redirect to loving and aligned action when you are clear on the very next step that is yours to take.

Create Space Spiritually

One of my most cherished activities is to sit next to the heat of a fire and I consider the process of building a fire to be a sacred one. Creating something as beautiful as a roaring, warm, light with small twigs, leaves, and the remnants of trees that once stood tall dancing in the wind has the power to heal, nurture, and invite reverence into our lives.

During the creation of this book, I woke up one morning with the intention of writing beside a new fire. As I began the activity of walking my yard, picking up what could be used as tinder, I became entwined with a mental dialogue that was taking place with my mother. My relationship with my mother had for years been a strained one, for various reasons, and recent events had awakened in me a great deal of pain. I was rightfully angry and valid in my emotions, but what began as reflections of how I could navigate the situation in love, quickly turned into blame, criticism, and judgment.

The most recent event to occur between us had opened a wound within me and I had been swirling for days in the raw emotions of residual and recent pains. Without awareness, I walked my yard picking up tinder, throwing it into my pit hastily, angrily, and with all the energy of how unfairly I had been treated. I lit it and relit it, over and over again, as judgements consumed me. Despite having gathered dry ingredients, my fire would not catch. After about thirty minutes or so, my soul caught up to me and I woke to how consumed I was with toxic energy.

I reentered the moment with deep sobs and returned my attention to my fire pit seeing for the first time the large pile of ash and soot beneath my newly laid tinder. I had been trying to build a new fire over the ashes of yesterday. In more ways than one, of course. Not only was I preventing my literal spark from catching, but my inner spark that was ready to create, was smothered by the bondage of past events and perceived wrong doings of my mother.

Creating space spiritually requires a practice that does not come easily to many, including myself. It is a practice that takes grace, courage, and compassion. Most of all it takes immense willingness to lay down the armor the ego uses as protection and let love envelope us instead. The practice of cultivating space spiritually is the intentional effort of letting go with none other than the F-word of spirituality... Forgiveness.

Forgiveness, I believe, is the highest expression of love. Forgiveness extends far beyond mere forgetfulness; it is a conscious surrender of judgments, expectations, and perceived wrongdoings into the loving embrace of God. Forgiveness is often associated with past events and individuals, yet it can also apply to present moment situations and the people around you - face to face, eye to eye, with whomever or whatever is before you. What I've come to realize is that when I harness forgiveness in this moment, when my mind might be deceiving me with judgements and criticism about myself, those around me, or the world - I am giving permission for love to enter my being, and not only does it touch the present moment, but it radiates to touch my past as well.

Forgiveness is giving love by letting go. Whether it be working toward letting go of anger and resentment, or simply having acceptance of others, despite their faults, forgiveness is how you create spiritual space within. It is also how you achieve sustainable stillness, by retraining your subconscious mind to stay attuned to the vitality of life.

As energetic beings, it does not serve our highest good to hold any aspect of life prisoner to our perceptions. In a society, where division and blame seem to prevail, we often overlook the fact that each person's perspective is shaped by their life experiences. As difficult as it may be to accept, each individual is making their way as best they can given the generational energy they carry and what they have lived through. As valid as it is to allow ourselves to feel emotional energy related to what is happening around us or the actions of another, it is also necessary for us to not be bound by those energetic ties. And so, to liberate ourselves from the shackles of discontent, forgiveness becomes essential.

It is important to note that forgiveness does not mean we agree with the actions of others or keep ourselves in toxic situations. It means acknowledging the current path of the individual or state of affairs while choosing to believe love exists in every moment and regardless of event specifics. This speaks to why the practice of forgiveness can be so difficult. Giving love means we must quite literally free ourselves and others of their errors and wrongdoings. In this way, we position ourselves to be channels of healing and hope by clearing out our own perceptions, so that space exists for a Higher Consciousness. A consciousness that is and only knows love.

My greatest call to forgive came to me when the recurring memory mentioned at the start of this chapter presented itself fully as I stood at my kitchen counter in April of 2020. After my friend and I laughed about the trunk slamming down on my left hand, she and I continued up the stone steps leading to the door of a house. This was the first new detail I was given. With fingers throbbing, she and I entered, setting our Burnett's raspberry vodka down on the kitchen island. I was then offered a pill for the pain before joining a small gathering of people.

That night, I was assaulted, but being accustomed to navigating life on my own and given my state of mind at the time, I didn't know how to respond. So, I convinced myself that nothing had happened. I pushed it down as far as I could in hopes of forgetting. What I know now is that nothing is ever really forgotten. The way I saw myself changed that night. I already felt like I didn't fully belong, and the events from this night made it harder to feel worthy or capable of anything good, a feeling I acted out in various ways for years afterward. I partied hard and lived carelessly, but, of course, the past lingered unseen.

When this memory, in its entirety, came back, I could see the many ways I had carried this burden with me. More than the self-inflicted destruction that immediately followed, I could see how I was still living in the aftermath of this event over 20 years later through the traces of shame, guilt, and anger I carried —anger about not being well nurtured when I was young, not being taught to value myself, not having anyone I could depend on, and being so naive and careless with how I treated my body. My continued work lies in recognizing for the sake of my freedom that I cannot go back in time. However, what I can do is love myself by lovingly handing over the uncontrollable nature of my past to God.

In this process, I recognize how counterintuitive it is to forgive people for physical, sexual, and emotional trauma because our reasoning mind wants them to suffer. However, the interconnected nature of our collective energy means that suffering cannot be confined to one person. When one person suffers, the collective experience of suffering is shared by all. This is evident in the cycles of violence, poverty, war, and destruction happening on our planet every day. Truth is, I will never know if the man who violated me will ever suffer as I once wished he would, but I do know that I will suffer if I continue to give my energy to those wishes.

A Course in Miracles says, "Forgiveness paints a picture of a world where suffering is over, loss becomes impossible and anger makes no sense. Attack is gone, and madness has an end."

Madness has an end.

My conscious decision to forgive is driven by a desire to end the madness within my mind, and it has led me to receive the highest form of love for myself. Since that day in April, I've committed to reshaping my mind's perspective on past events through embracing the power of forgiveness. My process for deep forgiveness involves prayer, participating in sweat lodge ceremonies, as well as, sharing my anger and sadness with the Earth because I recognize her as the ultimate Mother. I walk barefoot, sit, place my hands on the ground beneath me, and vocalize everything that is causing me suffering. I grieve as needed, releasing my pain and sorrow. As a result, I continue to experience new levels of compassion, freedom, and abundance.

There are two reasons why the energy of forgiveness is an ordered step in realizing stillness as a consciousness. The first is because forgiveness allows space for creative expression. Healing and creation go hand in hand. If I am consumed by the wrongs of what has happened to me, politics, the evil, naive and ignorant according to my perception, I will have no space within me to receive or manifest the desires living in the energy of my existence. If I am overly concerned with the error in warfare and the influence of plastics on our beautiful Earth, then rather than being available to whispers of heaven that offer abundant solutions, I will be consumed, angry, and burdened with fear. Moreover, I will be unable to experience this movement fully or move into my fullest expression as the hands and feet of a Higher Power.

The second reason why forgiveness holds significance is that every individual is born with a purpose. Given the self-regulating nature of the world, painful shifts in relationships and life events become necessary at times to fulfill that purpose. A crucial responsibility of the living is to contribute to healing ancestral energy, thus sparing future generations from carrying those same burdens. Presently, there's a growing awareness of this concept, reflected in terms like "cycle-breaker" and "trauma healing." It is important to recognize that if you have this awareness, your purpose is to heal generational suffering, to some extent, which does not come easily.

Sitting by the fire, grieving my relationship with my mother, I received the insight that she and I are on two very different journeys doing our part to heal brokenness within our lineage. I realized while there were many choices my mother made in my upbringing that were not the best, many aspects of her mothering were healed patterns of her upbringing. I recognize today that she did her part as best as she could to break cycles and now it is my turn to continue that journey as best as I can. With that understanding, what else is there to do but love?

As powerful as forgiveness is in healing relationships, forgiveness also opens channels of prosperity. One of the most memorable instances I experienced the prospering power of forgiveness happened in Fall of 2020 when absolutely nothing was going my way financially. I was particularly stressed and annoyed at the handful of meetings that did not result in clients. Though I had created space in other ways reflected in this chapter, I still felt stuck and financially strapped.

One day, I was sitting in my office and I remembered an insight shared by author and prosperity teacher Catherine Ponder. Catherine was ordained as a New Thought minister in 1958 in rural Alabama where she successfully taught laws of prosperity during economic depression. Her teachings helped countless participants prosper even throughout the dire appearance of worldly situations.

In one of her seminars, she said, "Many people are not permanently prosperous no matter what they do because they are holding grudges and negative feelings toward other people. This includes judgements about affluent people and people in office."

Through her work, she suggests that a good life requires a great deal of forgiveness and that we each should have a daily practice of "giving up" thoughts of inharmony. This was my cue to let go. I began writing down every person and event I could think of that I held a single bit of resentment or anger toward. My list ranged from individuals that had treated me unfairly, clients, family members, a rude customer service lady, Covid, the bills, my children, my husband, myself. I listed everything and everyone that came to my mind, whispering "*I fully and freely let go with love*" over and over again.

Soon thereafter, of course, freedom replaced the weight of the resentment I had been carrying and I was able to move forward blissfully, becoming the recipient of more than enough.

In my practice, I have found that creating space spiritually through forgiveness is beyond powerful and it begins by adapting a philosophy *for giving love* to everything that has offended you, which requires paying attention to what you are taking personally. As an observer, be mindful of criticisms, judgements, and condemnation held toward everyone and everything, however slight or major it may be. And I mean everything: the nail that punctured your tire, those who have hurt you, those who have taken lives, political leaders, the slow driver, your children, bill collectors, your partner, yourself, your parents, the spider that scared you, your bank account. Some of these things may sound silly, but grievances accumulate. So, regardless of the offenses' magnitude, giving love is how you create space to receive love in all the ways the universe wants to provide to you. Furthermore, because once again we are interconnected beings, the liberation that happens on an individual level, reaches the collective. There is no distance love cannot travel.

Forgiveness is an act of self-compassion that touches your soul, as well as the souls of those who came before and those who will come after you. It is among the highest of achievements to release the burden of blame, shame, and regret. Giving love to ourselves through the compassionate act of forgiveness transforms our current version of self into our highest expression of self.

Practice the Spiritual Law of Creating Space:

1. Forgive every person and event. Pay attention to criticism, judgements, condemnation, and any other feelings of offense. For every situation, see light surrounding the event. Release the habit of taking it personally. For every person that has offended you, see them happy, healthy, prospering, and living their best life. For those who have passed, see them smiling and dancing.

2. When feeling financially blocked, write down everything and everyone who could possibly need

forgiveness from you. Repeat, "I fully and freely let go with love. You are free and I am free too."

3. Create a relationship with the Earth and nature by sharing all that causes conflict and suffering within you. The Earth is a mother who nurtures all who walk upon her. When you feel deep emotions arising, stand outside barefoot if possible, touch a tree, or look up at the sky and breathe deeply while vocalizing all that you are experiencing.

CHAPTER 7

The Law of Co-Creation

*When I embrace the effort of seeing myself in the
highest possible way, when I have the courage to
reimagine who I am, who I am becoming, and what
I will create, miracles of the unseen realm are
natural occurrences.*

My shaman teacher shared that within the
Indigenous healing practice of Mesoamerican
tradition, called Curanderismo, it is believed that
inside each of us is "una guerra de las flores", *a war of
the flowers.* She says each of us brings wars of the
past into the present, but even so, we always have the
choice to see the past as an opportunity to create
beauty. She says, "You are the warrior that turns war
into beautiful flowers."

The Law of Creating Space is how you give love to the wars within and release all that you are fighting. The Law of Co-Creation is where you create beautiful flowers with those wars.

As we work through these Laws, you may have noticed that while they are written one at a time, they overlap and weave together. Rather than existing as a linear pattern, they flow akin to the perspective found in many Indigenous cultures, where the dynamics of the world unfold in a circle or wheel, with overlapping experiences and fluctuations of consciousness. This is especially true for the Law of Creating Space and the Law of Co-Creation, which offer unconfined experiences of healing and creation that occur in the present moment. By transforming stagnant energy or clutter across physical, mental, and spiritual realms, you open yourself right then and there to a renewed state of freedom through the creative power of your inner light.

As space is created within you, revelation takes place more often. You begin to unfold layers of worn-out thoughts, patterns, and most importantly unlearn old versions of self. Thereby, activating the ability to better hear the still small voice of your soul. Your intuition. Your inner guide.

As discussed in the previous chapter, revelation is the process of receiving information from a divine agency; it refers to the unveiling and uncovering of truths within. Through the Law of Creating Space, revelation is initially presented as memories or insights to aid in your walk of healing. However, as you persist in the practice of physical, mental, and spiritual clearing, revelation expands to unveil desires, dreams, and ideas aligned with your calling and your beautiful soul's work.

Though The Law of Co-Creation acknowledges our capacity to bring forth desires of the mind into the physical realm, it must be understood that the desires I'm speaking of are not necessarily materialistic manifestations, but instead encompass the inherent right you have to exist in such a way where external conditions never obstruct the flow of your prosperity, in all its many forms. This Law emphasizes the partnership between you and *all that is* —an agreement between your soul's purpose and universal supply.

Realizing The Law of Co-Creation begins by acknowledging your desires as a means through which God speaks to you. This means that when you accept them as real, all necessary provisions are supplied at the right and perfect time. Therefore, you must turn toward your desires and nudges, even when the question of "how?" exists. You must embrace them and nurture them and in doing so, the universe will nurture you. Hence the term co-creation.

Desires are revealed to us in two ways. The first are in the moments you catch glimpses of yourself doing things that fill your heart with excitement and possibility. These glimpses can reflect personal and professional achievements or intentions. It could be walking up to the front door of your new home, teaching a workshop, signing new clients, writing a book, expanding your friendship circle, doing your part to heal the planet, and much more. When acknowledged, you may notice yourself organically detaching from habits, certain foods, and relationships in pursuit of these desires.

The second way desires are revealed is through the presence of fear. Fear is an energy that manifests itself in various forms, ranging from anger and guilt or resentment, anticipation, and anxiety. In fact, any sensation that is not loving, peaceful, or bliss is fear. However, as gripping as the sensation of fear can be, within its grasp lies a curious beauty. Fear at its core, serves as a conduit to our desires.

Consider a time that you were gripped by fear, perhaps due to financial uncertainty. Your subconscious mind, wired for survival, employs fear as a signal, alerting you of this unresolved threat. In such moments, it's human nature to succumb to the downward spiral of inadequacy, especially if this is a circumstance you have encountered before. Yet, if you contemplated the fear you felt, you'd uncover the profound desire you have for abundance - the seamless flow of resources. Speaking power into this desire, which will be discussed later in this chapter, then becomes the rebel act.

Another example could be the worry or guilt you feel for someone close to you. Perhaps there's a person in your life whom you deeply love, yet you find yourself unable to assist them. They may be grappling with a challenging situation, and your concern for them weighs heavily on your mind. Despite fear's ability to deceive us into believing we have control over external circumstances, the reality is that our influence over others is limited. In the face of fear, our course of action may seem uncertain, but upon reflection, we can uncover a profound desire: to witness that person thriving—healthy, whole, joyous, and radiating in light and love. Seeing them experiencing life as such then becomes a solution within your control.

These revelations are how God speaks to you.

Your desires serve as a universal message of what is yours to experience and create by your transcendent right, as a child of the universe.

Yet, much more beautiful, is that when you accept your desires as a real part of your soul's purpose, you heal your lineage and honor your ancestors. You honor those that came before you, who had to fight and survive their own wars, to the best of their abilities. You also honor the generations after you. You are who your ancestors dreamed of and the desires you carry are the modern-day version of what they wished for you and for our planet.

Recognizing fear as a conduit of desire is how you transform the war within into flowers. By reframing fear through the lens of desire, rather than suppressing it, you reclaim agency. This shift changes the energetic frequencies coursing through your body from life defeating to life affirming. Thus, you become attuned to life's abundant possibilities, open to solutions within your reach. In essence, the transformation of fear into desire sparks a paradigm shift—one where limitations dissolve and your first step toward fulfilling that desire is found within the chaos.

Once you have become aware of the desires you hold, three experiences unfold within the Law of Co-Creation. First, a new concept of self is created. Second, guidance from the universe manifests. Third, you cultivate the ability to be pulled by vision, receiving signs along the way.

Align With A New Concept of Self

For most people, once a desire becomes clear, the tendency is to contemplate the potential of it based on external conditions or to embark on a quest to fulfill the desire through their own effort. Fueled by the subconscious mind's need for resolve, we begin planning, plotting, and taking exhaustive action, believing that these efforts will bring our desires to fruition. However, by imposing our will on our desires, we actually detract from the natural unfoldment of them, which inevitably leads to frustration and disappointment. This tendency to go at it alone, could be compared to asking someone for directions to a destination you're completely unfamiliar with, then choosing your own path without a map. Or having a conversation with someone you love deeply, only to walk away mid-sentence.

The universe does not wish that you work yourself hours on end to achieve the desire it has placed within you, but rather that you remain in constant communication, awaiting your next step. In the unseen realm, the co-creative relationship with Christ Consciousness is an ongoing and open dialogue. The flow of insights you receive related to your desires mirror that foundation. Just as it is with life partners, friends, colleagues, or children, we must embrace a willingness to collaborate.

The Law of Co-Creation emphasizes this collaboration by maintaining an open line of communication between you and God. This communication honors the rhythm of giving and receiving, which is how we keep the line open. We must always be willing to give first because we have been given free will. The ball, so to say, begins its dribble in our court. We give first by creating space within. We then receive the revelation of desire, a gift bestowed upon us by an omnipotent source—the gentle whisper of our soul.

The next gift we give involves our acknowledgment of our desires, embracing them as tangible and integral aspects of our life's purpose. This is done by aligning with a new concept of self. The best way to do this is with the vibratory power of your voice coupled with the oldest affirmation that exists, "I AM". I AM is how you embody the characteristics of God Mind.

In core Vedic texts that predate the finalization of the Hebrew Bible, the concept of I AM is embodied through the essence of So Hum, a Sanskrit mantra that translates to "I AM That" or "I AM He/She/ It". Though the exact phrase "So Hum" does not appear verbatim in these texts, it represents the unity of self with the universe. Each syllable of this mantra holds deep significance. In pranayama (breathing practices), "So" is associated with the breath entering the body, signifying the individual's connection to the

Holy One, while "Hum" is associated with the breath leaving the body, signifying the dissolution of the individual's ego as a means of creating unity with the universe.

The philosophy of I AM, however, is perhaps most widely recognized from the Biblical reference where it first appears in Exodus 3:14 when Moses asks for God to reveal himself by giving his name. In Hebrew, the name given is אֶהְיֶה אֲשֶׁר אֶהְיֶה, (ehye 'ăšer 'ehye). What's interesting about the translation of this word is that Biblical Hebrew does not distinguish between grammatical tenses. Therefore, the translation takes on many forms:

"I Am that I Am"
"I will become who I choose to become"
"I will be what I will be"
"I create whatever I create"
"I am the existing one."

Whether it be "So Hum" or scripture that resonates with you, the philosophy of "I AM" leads to an understanding that what we desire to create is intrinsically linked to our concept of self. Therefore, aligning with a new concept of self is how you elevate into the vibrational frequency that expands your potential to create. If you've ever tried to manifest prosperity in your life, you're probably familiar with affirmative prayer. You may have even declared to yourself statements that resemble the following:

"I AM wealthy"
"I create friendships with every person I meet"
"I AM safe"
"I create great value for my clients"

These statements, specifically when they are created in your own words, are gateways of communication with a self-organizing universe. The beginning of these statements "I AM", "I will be", "I create" serve as declarations of oneness with the omnipotent source within and the ending is anything you so choose. However, the power that exists within these statements is not only the words themselves, but the shift in consciousness that takes place within you. Over time, your feeling senses align with the new concept of self your words create and a magical process unfolds within your subconscious mind. The subconscious perceives what you have declared as a resolution and will initiate aligned action to support its realization.

Something that must be understood, however, is that the way in which our desires manifest is never completely revealed. If you look at the statements above, notice it is just as it is written in scripture, "In the beginning was the Word, and the Word was with God, and the Word was God" - "I AM". The ending is the intention fulfilled, but there is no middle. There is no blueprint for how your unfoldment will take place. For no other reason than the element of mystery that exists in the universe.

In 2017, when I was eight months pregnant with my youngest son, Roan, I experienced a memorable lesson in this. We traveled to the East Coast for a previously planned beach trip with friends. Months before, I had slowed my workload down and some unexpected financial hardships had developed. As a result, I experienced a dip in my commission, so I was particularly stressed on the drive down to the beach house and for the first two days of our trip. On the morning of the third day, realizing the state of my emotions led me to consider the double-mindedness I was experiencing, so I went outside on the balcony with an intention to shift the anxious thoughts. There was nothing that could be done while I was there and I wanted to enjoy the time I had with my oldest son and husband before we welcomed our newest member.

I sat on the balcony and after brain dumping and forgiving everything and everyone I could think of, I began to write a lengthy declaration of who I AM.

This is what I wrote:

October 6, 2017

Today, I AM shifting my mind and embracing myself as a renewed woman and mother. I am a loving and present mother. I embrace vulnerability and make friends everywhere I go. I am a present business owner. I live with an open heart and the right and perfect people gravitate toward me. I am open to unexpected miracles. I allow worries, fears, anything and anyone that does not serve my highest good to dissipate, reclaiming the Truth that I am in perfect harmony with universal substance. I remain thankful for all the moments in my life, even those that seem scary. I will remember daily that good exists in all experiences. I release my future with confidence that all things are working together for the greater good of all. I love paying bills on time, tithing, and giving generously. I love welcoming new clients, entering in agreements, and giving great service. I love spending time with my family and traveling. I am a woman that people look forward to seeing. I love being congratulated for accomplishments and sharing in the celebration of others. I am the woman who looks her children in their eyes and makes play and laughter a priority, even when scary situations are present.

I AM a blissful and prosperous woman.

I read and reread these words aloud until I felt anxiety transform and the exhilarating feeling of confidence that takes place with realignment arise in my being. I experienced what A Course in Miracles refers to as a Holy Instant. A moment in time that teaches us the meaning of love by suspending judgment of past or future experiences.

"The Holy Instant", A Course in Miracles says, "is a time in which you receive and give perfect communication. This means, however, that it is a time in which your mind is open, both to receive and give. It is the recognition that all minds are in communication. It therefore seeks to change nothing, but merely to accept everything."

After my time on the balcony, I was elevated into the new concept of self I had created. I was able to join my family with joy, excitement, patience, and all the qualities I had declared for myself. I was able to accept everything as it was and just be present.

The following day, I received an email from a man who worked within the same company as I did, but in a different territory. Though I had no direct experience with him, I was aware that he was someone many people within our company had complained about. He had left a bad impression on both clients and colleagues. There was even an active effort taking place to boot him from the company.

The email he sent was to inform me that he had just made a very large sale to a client that would be under my management. I can't stress enough how unexpected it was to receive a demonstration of abundance through this man.

Yet as incredible as it was to receive this gift, what was more exciting was the deep knowing that settled within me:

When I embrace the effort of seeing myself in the highest possible way. When I have the courage to reimagine who I AM, who I AM becoming, what I will create, miracles of the unseen realm are a natural occurrence.

This is a universal law set into motion by the shift in your consciousness and when your statements of "I AM" are said frequently, with the vibratory power of your voice, all the better.

As humans, we have the unique ability to create through the vibratory power of our voice. Many of the greatest spiritual revolutionaries proclaim power of the spoken word as the greatest instrument of change. The concept of the spoken word dates to preliterate history, predating the written word, and is widely referenced in many spiritual texts.

Isaiah 55:11 says, "So shall my word be that goes out from my mouth; it shall not return to me empty, but it shall accomplish that which I purpose, and shall succeed in the thing for which I sent it."

"Raise your word", the Persian poet Rumi said, "not voice - it is rain that grows flowers, not thunder."

In a scientific study conducted by Japanese scientist, Dr. Masaru Emoto, it was found that vocal vibrations shape water's molecular structure. Using high-speed photography and vibration measuring devices, he observed water responding to sound vibrations. Positive words yielded beautiful crystals, while negative ones led to distorted shapes. This highlights water's memory and impact on life. He further reported that our words have a direct impact on human consciousness, given that the human body is 70% water.

Of course, the Shamans of our world have known this for ages. I've learned from various teachers the power of speaking prayers into water before drinking it as a way of cleansing and empowering the energy I carry.

Well known psychoanalyst, Sigmund Freud once said, "Words have magical power. They can either bring the greatest happiness or the deepest despair." Therefore, it's vital to speak positively about ourselves and others, as our words shape our reality.

One last important consideration is to write down your desires, even those that are superficial. The desires not meant to be, will be cleared away until only the deep desires remain. This insight helps to avoid fixating on specific material manifestations and their origins. While it's common to perceive circumstances, institutions, or individuals as the sources of our blessings, genuine prosperity encompasses flourishing circumstances, favorable outcomes, and success across all dimensions of life, including relationships, health, and personal development. Solely fixating on specific manifestations can unintentionally restrict the potential for abundant outcomes from unseen sources.

Instead, dedicate your energy to reimagining yourself as the loving parent, successful author, or creative business owner you aspire to be. Frequency attracts frequency, therefore by feeling into your highest concept of self, people, opportunities, financial abundance, and material manifestations matching the resulting frequency will gravitate to you with ease.

Whispers from the Unseen Realm

Surrendering the need to know how things will unfold presents a great challenge for many of us. This difficulty arises because faith requires entrusting control of outcomes to an unseen power and embracing peace and joy in the present moment, regardless of outer influences. Peace and joy are frequencies that some may not be accustomed to, as they believe these qualities come at a cost, rather than being our inherent privilege.

This is why declaring your desired state of I AM is so important and must be a daily practice if you do not wish yourself to be at the mercy of the world. In fact, it should evolve into a deeply ingrained habit for each of us to better overcome sensations of suffering. Over time, as you anchor yourself in your desired state of being, you'll observe a transformation in your outer world.

This shift is what ultimately elevates your energy to a higher frequency, allowing you to transcend the limitations of the physical world and tap into the boundless supply of the spiritual realm. As it is stated in Romans 12:2, "Do not conform to the pattern of this world, but be transformed by the renewing of your mind. Then you will be able to test and approve what God's will is—his good, pleasing and perfect will." Or as I translate it, you will know what the inner voice of your soul is guiding you to fulfill. You will know what is right and true for your journey.

As I mentioned earlier, we are never handed the complete roadmap for fulfilling our soul's work, even when we have a clear vision of the desired outcome. This is because the universe is in a constant state of flux. It rises and falls. It heals and nurtures. All movements exist within the framework of the present moment. However, even without knowing the complete path to fulfillment, we are gifted with signs along the way, affirming that we are indeed on the right track.

This leads us to the next experience that arises within the Law of Co-Creation and that is the occurrence of synchronicities. Synchronicities are magical and mysterious moments that signal alignment and forward movement toward our desires.

118

As you seek revelation and accept who you are in God Mind, you invite mystery into your life, leading to a cascade of interconnected moments that defy simple explanation. This phenomenon is encapsulated by the term Synchronicity. It means to experience meaningful coincidences that on the surface may seem unrelated, but spiritually offer confirmation that the lines of communication are open and you are in alignment with universal supply.

The philosophy of synchronicity was developed by psychologist and researcher Carl Jung, who not only introduced the concept but also coined the term 'synchronicity'. According to Jung, synchronicities reflect deep psychological processes and convey messages much like dreams do.

The roots of meaningful coincidence, however, extend far beyond Jung's philosophy. Over three thousand years prior, ancient Chinese philosophy believed seemingly random events possess inherent significance. One of the most renowned artifacts associated with this is the I Ching oracle, also known as The Book of Changes, which has provided guidance for decision-making in philosophies of Confucianism, Taoism, and Buddhism for centuries. Legend has it that Fuxi, an enlightened ancient Chinese world leader and originator of divination methods, created eight trigrams or symbols by observing patterns in the natural world. Each trigram, composed of three horizontal lines, symbolizes the interplay of yin and yang energy inherent in all phenomena.

The divination process of the I Ching involves a synchronistic exchange by first asking a question, then through the generation of seemingly random numbers, one can find meaning in associated readings. Other divination methods aligning with synchronicity in modern times include tarot or oracle cards, cowrie shell divination, horoscopes, and astrology.

The presence of synchronicity, whether it be through divination practices or seemingly random events, is another way the universe speaks to us, reminding us of our connection to a Higher Power. Metaphysically, synchronicities suggest that our souls draw people and events to us so that we may evolve in consciousness. I've found this to be especially true when we welcome unfoldment. This invitation enhances our ability to receive confirmation from the spiritual world.

Synchronicities are gentle whispers from the universe, reassuring you that you're not alone, affirming that you're on the right path, and providing support for the decisions you're making, the insights you're receiving, and the grace you're granting yourself. Whether it's repeatedly encountering the same numbers, noticing the clock at a consistent time each day, unexpectedly meeting someone after thinking about them, or reflecting on a significant life event and then encountering a meaningful symbol, synchronicities manifest in various ways, but resonate on an individual level.

The story of finding my eagle pipe, where the symbol of an eagle presented itself many times in a way that resonated with my core, is one of my favorite synchronistic events. However, there isn't a day that goes by that I don't experience communication and connection through coincidences. When I was still learning to accept these instances, there was often a lot more emotion involved. Now, it's simply a matter of tuning in to what I would like to happen or what I think I could have done better, and then waiting for the solution to be presented or to receive confirmation that all is well.

For instance, years ago when I was beginning to really pay attention and accept messages, there was one day I was driving to a coffee shop to work on a talk I was giving. I had been contemplating this talk and feeling consumed with self-doubt. I thought to myself "What am I doing?" and "Am I really capable of this?".

Though I rarely listen to the radio these days, on this day my car radio was playing in the background when a song came on that I hadn't heard in months, maybe even years—so long that I had forgotten about it. The song was "Home" by Edward Sharpe and the Magnetic Zeros. The line I love most is, "Home, let me come home. Home is wherever I'm with you." Overall, it's one of those songs that, when I hear it, feels like a kiss from spirit—an inner surge of chills that rises from deep within, touches my skin, and warms my heart.

As soon as I became aware of the song, this is what I felt and by the time the song ended, the anxious energy had transformed into excitement. I resolved that when it came time for my talk, I would simply be at *home* on stage. This song served me as a return to a Holy Instant, helping me to suspend my judgments and attachments to what my future held and I was absolutely elated.

I then arrived at the coffee shop. As I got settled in the booth and I opened my computer, the instrumental version of the same song began to play through the cafe's speakers.

Even as I write this, remembering that moment in time, I feel the kiss of spirit. This for me was confirmation that I had received the message that was meant for me. It was also a reminder that as long as I am willing to seek help and validation from the universe, I will always be supported.

Another example occurred during a recording of my podcast, "Rooted in Purpose with Jess and Tamara", which I co-host with a friend in Canada. Before recording, we noticed that our guest was nervous about sharing her message. We both offered insight and words of encouragement, reminding her that we were there for connection, not perfection. As we were speaking to her, I felt a gentle nudge from my heart to offer a prayer, but I wasn't sure how it would be received, so I hesitated. Seconds later, Tamara said, "We're all believers of a Higher Power and being of service to our gifts." I took this as my timely cue and made my offer, which was well received and exactly what we needed.

Later, during the same interview, another moment of support through synchronicity occurred. I had elaborated on an idea our guest had mentioned but forgot to follow up with a specific question. As the interview continued, I was concerned if I'd be able to ask it without disrupting the flow, but I remained open that the right moment would present itself. As we reached the end of our time, Tamara asked our guest if there was anything else she'd like to share. Her answer was completely aligned with my question.

Now, of course, there are skeptics who resist giving meaning to coincidences, but I hope you won't be one of them. Instead, I hope you allow yourself to consider the meaning within events that remind you to follow your heart. You are the light that you seek. Let it be so, and synchronicities will teach you to trust yourself and the messages brought to you by your beloved soul.

Be Pulled by Vision

The next phase of The Law of Co-Creation involves being pulled by vision, a concept distinct from the practice of visualization. While both have their place in the journey of spiritual unfoldment, it's crucial to distinguish between the two. Visualization, often associated with manifesting and bringing what is outside of us into our world, includes techniques such as vision boards, affirmative daydreaming, and guided imagery. This powerful practice expands our mental capacity through conscious imagination, helping us create new neural pathways. It also enhances our ability to sustain prosperity and to accept positive manifestations and new experiences into our lives.

In contrast, being pulled by vision, or the practice of visioning, brings what already exists within us to the surface. Rather than consciously creating images in our minds, it involves receiving glimpses of where we are headed. This phenomenon comes as a feeling, accompanied by deeper intuition and sometimes an image. All of these elements are connected to our purpose and all of which are presented in a timely manner according to the self-organizing power of the universe.

When you receive a glimpse of yourself doing something that you have aspired to do it is confirmation that the dreams and passion you carry within are not idle fantasies. They are intrinsic to your being, part of your DNA, and meant for you to pursue. Visioning validates these innate aspirations.

Whether it be a desire to write a book, have peace in your relationships, release addiction, visions show you where you are headed. You are engaged with visioning when you see, in your mind's eye, glimpses or whispers that you are not actively creating or imagining. These are messages connected to your purpose. They are universal desires woven into the fabric of your being. Therefore, it is safe to assume everything you could possibly need will be provided to you in the realm of spiritual time.

Spiritual time is another important concept to understand when it comes to co-creation because in modern day society, time is often viewed as our most limited resource, especially when pursuing a goal. The construct of time can seem like an unyielding force that we are up against. Sayings such as "time waits for no one", "better three hours too soon than a minute too late", "time is the most valuable thing a man can spend", and so on portray time as an objective measurement.

Much of this has to do with the evolution of timekeeping, which began more than 5,000 years ago, with the Babylonians. In that era, time was created to measure the transition of day to night, to better move with the fluctuations of the earth, for planting and harvesting crops, even to conceive. Calendars were influenced by three cycles: the solar day, signified by periods of light and dark created as the earth rotates on its axis. The lunar month that regards the phases of the moon as it orbits the earth. The solar year which considers the changing seasons as our planet revolves around the sun.

From these early calendar systems, the concept of measured time continued to develop, with the Egyptians who devised a calendar consisting of 12 months, each with 30 days, as well as measuring intervals of darkness, which are called temporal hours. Temporal hours were subsequently adopted by the Greeks and Romans, who spread the technology throughout Europe and influenced the development of timekeeping systems across various cultures.

The migration of timekeeping information spurred the advancement of clock technology, notably with the Roman Catholic Church. In the 8th and 9th century, utilizing time measurement, the Church established a structured prayer schedule, employing bells to signal prayer times to surrounding communities. This happening offers an interesting reflection regarding the interplay between objective and spiritual time because it points to a moment in history where outer direction was given for a practice of inner connection.

It also brings another light to my Cherokee Elders words, "At some point in history, we learned to let time tell us when we're hungry..." or we learned to let others tell us when and how to pray, create, live.

Fast forward to the present day, timekeeping has evolved from a relationship with nature, the moon, harvesting crops, and creating community into numerous systems designed to precisely measure and plan the duration of events. To the extent that most individuals adhere to the structure of calendars and rigid schedules for instruction regarding daily matters, as well as the unfoldment of their desires.

While there is certainly a need for measured time and as much as you'd like to set specific plans and goals when honoring a vision you have received you are collaborating with the universe, which works in mysterious ways and on its own time.

The reason we do not experience instant gratification in achieving our desires is that we must grow into our new concepts of self, which is a gradual process. This growth requires patience and trust in spiritual timing. By embracing this truth, we allow ourselves to evolve naturally, creating the space to sustain our manifestations.

Embodying spiritual time is especially futile for parents. The role of raising children has been sidelined in modern society, but it is the most important role in the world. It goes beyond and above everything. Many parents have a vision of themselves creating a loving life for their children. Yet often we put our work first thinking that is what matters because it produces tangible results in real time. But, just like our work, our children are channels of abundance. Acknowledging this with your presence, is how parents can shift into spiritual time - where nothing divine is ever lost.

When desires are pulling you, remembering that desire comes from spirit can help you embrace spiritual timing, and know that even when you can't see progress happening on the surface, if you are permitting yourself to move toward joy, you are moving forward.

I first began receiving glimpses of speaking, writing, and sharing spiritual ideas around the age of 14, which I initially dismissed as idle thoughts because I had not yet grown into the version of myself that resonated with these visions. In fact, it wasn't until 25 years later that I began to accept them as my destiny. The path to fully embracing that involved passing through a great deal of trauma, a dark night of the soul and a global pandemic, all of which I could have never predicted.

When I finally stepped onto this path in mid-2020, I was terrified of so many things, including our financial situation and working to stabilize my business. Yet, I had a deep longing to write and glimpses of this book fluttered through my mind. I did what many people do when a desire is revealed. I allowed my will to interfere. Rather than waiting for guidance, I began planning on exactly how I was going to write this book while juggling my business. I even marked a date on my calendar, determined to will it into existence, on my own terms.

However, it wasn't long before I found myself struggling to strike a balance, often prioritizing work tasks over my creative pursuits due to feelings of guilt and fear. As a result, when I did find time to write, it wasn't with joy but with a sense of urgency. Needless to say, I exhausted myself in the process. I reached a breaking point one day driving home that changed my entire outlook on manifestation.

On this day, I was spiraling out, an emotional mess, tears streaming down my face. All I wanted was confirmation that the vision of me writing this book was real. As I was driving, I said aloud, "Just show me this is real and I'll do it. I'll trust the pull to write. I'll trust this is mine to do." Without even thinking, I said, "Show me a hawk".

I then took a curve to the left and straight in front of me, I immediately noticed a bird flying above a light post. I tapped on my breaks, awestruck, and squinted my eyes to get a better view. To this day, I can tell you, the bird flying above was a hawk, but on that day, there was too much distance between me and *that bird*, I was not convinced. I resumed my drive, saying aloud, "You're going to have to do better than that. I need to know without a doubt that this is real."

The road curved again, leading to a stop sign where I turned right once more. Tall trees lined the road, and as I approached them, a magnificent red-tailed hawk emerged, gliding directly over my open sunroof. Its wings outstretched, displaying vibrant specks of red and brown. I was left speechless, knowing without a doubt this was a genuine sign that I was on the right path.

One thing to know about asking for a sign and honoring vision is to understand that whatever comes into your mind, it is not from you, but from spirit. The contents of this book and even the idea of asking for a hawk was not something I consciously made up, it's all revelation: information provided by a divine agency, *pulling me into formation* and oneness with God.

With my confirmation that day, I surrendered to my desire and embraced a pace dictated not by will or perceived urgency, but by the gentle rhythm of my soul's longing to evolve into higher states of being. I accepted my vision with presence and as a result witnessed the universe's organizing power at work. Opportunities, emails, new clients flowed to me effortlessly—even amid a pandemic.

Another important takeaway I gained is the understanding that growing into our abundance is how we create sustainable prosperity. We have all manifested one thing or another, from time to time, but true and sustainable prosperity comes from evolving our vibration through ordered action. The downfall of relying solely on visualization is that instead of allowing what lies within us to naturally arise, we impose our will upon our destiny, hindering our soul's natural unfoldment.

The Law of Co-Creation invites us to embrace mystery and experience miracles as a natural occurrence by communicating with universal intelligence. Embracing this awareness aligns us with spiritual time, where guidance unfolds effortlessly through synchronicity. In this journey, there's no need to hesitate in seeking confirmation—it's a vital aspect of our growth and spiritual evolution.

CHAPTER 8

The Law of Celebration

Through the abundant power of praise and prayer, I now cultivate a deeper capacity to celebrate every moment on my path toward earthly happiness and spiritual joy, unaffected by worldly events or the actions and words of others.

Navigating the pursuit of our dreams often involves confronting moments when the path ahead seems unclear or when life doesn't unfold as we imagined. A common pitfall when these moments arise is presuming failure to be on the horizon or doubting the dreams we carry. I believe this is because society has lost touch with the movement of nature, the dips, and the sorrow that is part of life and renewal. In addition, opinions associated with modern day practices of manifestation suggest that we must always be happy in order to realize our desires. As a result, we tend to think that when we're following our purpose or doing what is good, everything is going to go our way. This belief arises even as we embrace The Law of Co-Creation, opening ourselves to signs and the visions we carry. We think that because we are now in pursuit of our soul's work, outcomes will go as expected on a happy uphill journey.

The issue at hand with this mentality, is that when obstacles or thoughts we don't like do present themselves, as they surely will, there is a tendency to become resistant to these challenges or think we've done something wrong. Perhaps because we were not positive or grateful enough. This way of thinking resonates with the Law of Attraction, a philosophy that suggests just as positive thoughts bring forth positive results, negative thoughts bring forth negative results. While positive thoughts can be attractive and produce fleeting happiness, I find this particular aspect of the philosophy constrictive to spiritual unfoldment because it encourages that we suppress negative thoughts. Suppression does not serve our highest good because all thoughts are energy that must be allowed space to transform.

Though happiness is a natural state of our being, we also encounter a vast spectrum of other emotions because life is unpredictable and rarely smooth sailing. We also experience intrusive thoughts despite whether we agree with them or not. Therefore, it is important to acknowledge all energy as it arises. This is especially true when pursuing your soul's work, as adverse situations and self-sabotaging thoughts may seem more frequent. This perception arises not because they are, but because your subconscious, lacking a blueprint for the future, is attempting to protect you from the unknown that you are more frequently embracing.

Furthermore, since you have made a choice to welcome healing into your pursuit of creation, you have also developed a greater awareness of what is out of alignment with your soul's essence than you had before. Therefore, whatever is out of alignment will emerge awaiting resolution.

The Law of Celebration follows the Law of Co-Creation because it encourages us to unlearn the habit of perceiving failure when we encounter obstacles. The propensity to do this is common amongst us and has a great deal to do with how we view success and failure overall. Just as we see emotions as either positive or negative, we tend to attach the label of success or failure to our experiences. If we have an experience that we perceive to be successful, it is cause for celebration and happiness, so we reserve celebration for special occasions. Likewise, happiness, which by its standard definition means to have a content mental state due to experiencing advantageous circumstances, is only possible when external conditions or outcomes have met our perceptions of success.

The core dilemma is that external conditions will never be perfect. Therefore, you cannot have happiness without pain. This awareness points to the lesson learned in the previous chapter about seeing fear energy as guideposts for what you desire. When an obstacle presents itself, before labeling it as a threat, search within for what you'd love to see happen instead. Since healing and creation unfold in a reciprocal nature, all emotional energy is important to the sustainability of stillness and abundance. Thus, the key is to learn how to let emotional energy heal and transform within you, rather than react or suppress.

The beautiful teacher and author Thich Nhat Hahn referred to this idea with his philosophy of learning to suffer well. He says, "One of the most difficult things for us to accept is that there is no realm where there's only happiness and there's no suffering... If we focus exclusively on pursuing happiness, we may regard suffering as something to be ignored or resisted. We think of it as something that gets in the way of happiness. But the art of happiness is also and at the same time the art of knowing how to suffer well. If we know how to use suffering, we can transform it and suffer much less."

In pursuit of embracing stillness as a consciousness, I have found reassessing my criteria for celebration to be vital. Rather than attempting to maintain constant happiness, shifting my perception to meet challenges with peace and rest has allowed me to realize that sometimes celebration is the rebel act. Celebration is a humble gesture that gives strength to life, while communicating to the universe what we'd like to experience more of before moving on to the next thing.

The Law of Celebration teaches us how to expand our capacity for joy and is a powerful catalyst for transformation because it looks beyond the goal of fleeting happiness, aiming instead for enduring bliss, which is to experience earthly happiness and spiritual joy. The lessons learned through this Law is an accumulation of all the Laws before it. The Law of Celebration invites us to welcome oneness where there is separation, forgive attachment to outcomes, timelines, and perceived error in ourselves and others, and learn to celebrate both successes and failures - through the practice of praise and prayer.

Speak to the Soul with Praise

My first memorable instance of experiencing the power of praise, regarding another person, occurred when I was 20 and living on my own in Nashville, Tennessee. I was working at a dance studio, teaching ballroom dance, in a toxic and judgmental environment. Though I didn't have many friends at the studio, there was one female dance teacher in particular who really did not like me. She would flat out ignore me when I spoke and talk about me behind my back.

One Friday night as I was driving home, I pondered this woman's behavior with an especially colorful mix of words. While I was perfectly content to not be her friend, it bothered me a great deal to be on the receiving end of energy that I did not welcome and I found myself sending that same energy back to her in my mind. As I thought about our interactions, I heard clearly, "speak to her soul with praise".

Excuse me?

I was completely caught off guard by these words. Understandably so because obviously… What was there to praise? I had given her many chances to reciprocate my kindness and she had let me down each time. Why and for what reason should I praise her?

I'm sure you can relate to how I was feeling. Dealing with people who have caused us harm, misled us, or simply annoyed us can be challenging. It's hard to have empathy for those who have brought about negative emotions or experiences. For this reason, praise and celebration are often reserved for when we are receiving what we want from others. However, the word praise means to attach value to something. It means to lift up, to rejoice, to acknowledge value in others. In religious context, praise is a word often directed to a God outside of ourselves, but in spiritual context, praise acknowledges God in all. Therefore, it is a powerful tool for inviting good into the present moment, even when no good is in sight. What you praise is what you invite into your world.

"Speak to her soul with praise," I heard again. What I understood this to mean was that, beyond mere forgiveness, I was to consciously choose to see her in a positive light. After a bit of resistance, I began speaking words of praise. I celebrated her abundance, health, and joyous experiences. I said aloud, yet at first begrudgingly, "I praise your divine spark, Charlotte. I see you happy and prosperous. I see you making money and living your best life. You are a talented dancer and I see you attracting the right and perfect clients. I see you with healthy relationships. I am rooting for you and all the good you will do and experience."

As I continued, my begrudging attitude shifted to happiness and my energetic body was lifted through the favor I was giving Charlotte. Over the weekend, I continued this practice each time she entered my mind by taking a few seconds to celebrate her innate goodness. When Monday came around, I went into the studio with zero regard for past interactions and was simply at peace with the day.

That morning, I had a meeting with a client who was frustrated about the conditions of a dance package she bought, so I was discussing the options with her at the front desk. The conversation was at first heavy and I came to find out my client was experiencing a financial bind. Eventually we got around to a solution and ended with humor. At some point during the exchange, Charlotte had come to the front desk (which she never did while I was there) and as my client was leaving, something funny was said that caused us both to look at each other and laugh.

On the inside I was floored. We had never had an interaction like that. It was as if a switch had been flipped and from that day on, we were on good terms. There was no in person conversation about why we weren't before or what happened between us. It was simply divine resolution.

I have learned that in relation to others, praise realigns us with one-mindedness because it dispels disillusionment. Often, we become disillusioned by the actions and words of others and it is the subconscious mind's resolution to condemn them so that we might protect ourselves. Instead, however, by fixating on what we can't stand in another person, we cause ourselves suffering and this is a behavior that has become yet another generational habit we must break.

A Course in Miracles refers to this idea as accepting guilt into the mind. It says that any form of attack toward another person stems from our own belief of unworthiness. Instead of facing this belief directly, our subconscious deflects it by pointing fingers at others in an effort to create a false sense of separation, leading to disharmony and offense. This is a significant illusion because as energetic beings, we are interconnected, therefore it is impossible for me to hurt you without hurting myself and vice versa.

Thus, we must pay extra attention to how we are attending to situations regarding other people. Whether it be that they are casting judgment on us or their own circumstances and the other way around. Realizing through this awareness that as interconnected beings, it is our responsibility to uplift, cherish, and celebrate the light within one another if humanity is to survive.

Thich Nhat Hanh said, "We have to train ourselves to look in a way so that we know when we touch one thing, we touch everything. We have to see that the one is in the all, and the all is in the one."

Celebration through the practice of praise is how we illuminate the world. Praise is the exquisite act of acknowledging the brilliance within others, reshaping our perception of them, and revering the divine essence that animates us, present within them. It is how we connect soul to soul. Just as our own light can be dimmed by traumas and sorrows, so too can our neighbors', whether they live next door, in distant countries, or rule nations. It encompasses our parents, siblings, friends, exes, and all those who have caused us pain or been on the receiving end of our condemnation. Through words that redefine their essence in our minds, we energetically uplift them. In this exchange of love, both giver and receiver are elevated.

Lowell Fillmore, an author and teacher of the early 1900's New Thought movement, referred to this concept as renaming your enemies. In his book New Ways to Solve Old Problems, he says we have a habit of continually naming and renaming people around us. We name them beautiful, graceful, awkward, difficult, honest, liar, bad, ugly, and so on. The names we pick for people are based on impressions made in our experiences with them. When someone interferes with our plans, we alter our mental picture of who they are, and change how we identify them in a way that contributes to negativity in our mind.

Lowell suggests that if you want to change someone's behavior, you must first change the mental image you hold of them by giving them a better name. This should not be done with the intention of trying to make them over, but rather to bring more good into your own world. Meaning that in this process of elevation, anyone that does not meet the frequency you are creating with your words, will find no place in your world and naturally drift away on their own. He further says, "It is your divine privilege to name the people who live in your mental world so that they will be helpful to you. Fill your world with good and helpful people by your power to name them with good names. You cannot afford to have bad people about you, and you do not need to have them. The old-fashioned way to get rid of enemies was to kill them, spirit them away, or lock them up. The modern, Christ way to dispose of enemies is to transform them into friends and helpers. To do this you must cease to worry about their shortcomings."

In other words, when dealing with unpleasant people, instead of complaining or shaming them, redirect the energy spent on negative emotions and choose to see them in a different light. This goes for all people, especially world leaders, familial ties where identities can be deeply rooted, and any relationships that require healing. Regarding the latter, there is no need to stay in the lives of these individuals, but we still must avoid excessive venting or gossip at all costs, as it fills our minds, bodies, and souls with toxic energy. Even engaging in internal dialogues that replay scenarios where we feel unfairly treated perpetuates negativity within us.

Instead, take your concerns to the Earth, whisper them to the wind, place them in water, or release them to fire and when feelings of envy arise as you witness the accomplishments of others, be happy for them. What the universe has done in the lives of others, can also be done in yours. It is an unchanging truth that when abundance happens for others, abundance is close to happening for you.

The Power of Prayer

Whether it's an interaction with another person or a challenging circumstance, The Law of Celebration encourages us to redirect our energy with the intention of elevating our mind, body, and spirit connection as we move toward experiencing authentic joy in every situation. Just as we must learn to rename our enemies, we must also learn to rename our circumstances. The lessons of The Law of Celebration, particularly concerning external conditions, involve recognizing double-mindedness and redefining our perceptions of success and failure through the practice of prayer.

The first lesson begins with the realization that all human beings are hard wired with what is known as negative bias, which is an expression of our double-minded nature. A negative bias is the tendency to register negative stimuli more readily than we do positive. It is also the habit of giving more weight to things that could go wrong than what could go right.

Negative bias is yet another cause of suffering because it demonstrates that regardless of the situation at hand, we are likely to perceive and act upon our negative perceptions. Studies suggest this is because there is a significant surge of electrical activity in the human brain when it encounters negative stimuli. This surge creates a strong pull that, without awareness, can cause our behaviors and attitudes to be shaped more significantly by bad news and negative or non-essential information than positive.

The influence of negative bias has greatly increased with the rising presence of technology, social media, and smartphones. These devices create a means of instant gratification as our brains experience surges of dopamine and serotonin. As a result, we have learned to quickly move from one thing to another, easily distracted and often resistant to receiving guidance and accepting spiritual time.

In everyday life, negative bias is why we are quick to see what went wrong or what mistakes have been made by ourselves or someone else, rather than acknowledging accomplishments. It explains why people have a hard time releasing trauma and why we are drawn to negative news. Other examples include the vivid memories we carry of humiliating past events or our tendency to replay criticism, in our mind, rather than compliments. It is also why we are quick to move through our achievements, with little to no celebration.

Ultimately, our ingrained tendency toward negative bias, compounded by the influence of technology, prevents us from experiencing enduring bliss, peace of mind, and rest whenever we desire. To counter this negative bias in a way that promotes well-being, I've found more helpful than simple mindfulness is the power of prayer.

Prayer is another word that some people can have resistance toward, usually because of religious affiliation. The word prayer, at its PIE roots, means to ask or entreat, which is to plead or beg with urgency. Since the 14th century, the word prayer has been used to describe the act of worship and devout petition to God, as an outside entity.

However, the word prayer was initially meant to provide a translation for the Hebrew word תפילה (Tefillah), which takes on an entirely different meaning. Rather than a practice that regards two entities, ourselves as inferior, making a request to a superior being, Tefillah means to account for, contemplate, and execute judgment by communicating your deepest wishes, desires, and concerns to the Holy One. It is yet another avenue of communication. According to Hebrew scripture, Tefillah is not a commandment but a gift from a Higher Power, allowing us to commune with Divine presence, remaining aware of our ongoing oneness.

Prayer, when viewed in terms of Tefillah, is an essential aspect of The Law of Celebration because it offers peace of mind in moments of concern and extended joy in moments we wish to savor more deeply. Prayer plays a significant role when cultivating a consciousness of stillness and experiencing enduring bliss because it is a pathway of surrender, helping us to detach from distractions and outcome.

The reason prayer is important when it comes to celebration is because it activates our connection with ancestors, angels, and universal intelligence. Prayer is how we invite what exists beyond what we see with our physical eyes into our current situation. Whether it be to help us release our distracted mind or solve a hardship, we need the gift of prayer to escape the limited lens of our impulsivities and expectations.

Once you begin embracing the Law of Co-Creation, you will find that prayer is invaluable in creating the life you desire. Its power to inspire and realign your inner world with surrounding abundance will keep you continually seeking to maintain open lines of communication with the universe.

This is what my husband and I experienced one Spring, as we were looking for a vehicle that he could trade for the broken down jeep he had been driving for years. When we began our search, we asked that the perfect choice be made obvious to us. A few days later, we were so excited that we acted quickly to purchase a used SUV, within our small budget, near perfect condition and with low mileage. After taking the vehicle home, we went to search for a warranty that would cover any sort of powertrain issues that could occur with any used vehicle. We were surprised to find that this SUV had a transmission different from the typical automatic transmissions we were used to and no warranty seemed to cover it.

Understandably anxious, my husband called the dealership and several additional warranty companies to find a solution. When no solutions were forthcoming, I told my husband we should take a second and pray.

It was on a Tuesday that we sat close together, holding hands as I said, "Mother, Father, God, we aren't quite sure if we've made the right choice here. If we weren't listening before, we are listening now. We are asking for guidance to find a solution so that we may be able to truly enjoy and celebrate this vehicle, or something better. We invite our ancestors and angels to join us and guide us as we communicate clearly with the dealership our concerns and we ask they have an open heart to hear. We don't know how it will look, but we are so thankful for all the good being born in this moment. Amen. It is done."

After our prayer, we were able to fully surrender knowing there was nothing left for us to do, and trusting that a solution would present itself by Thursday, when we had scheduled another visit to the dealership.

That Thursday, I was tied up with a deadline and couldn't accompany my husband to the dealership as early as we planned. Despite our worry of showing up too late in the afternoon when dealership managers might be busy helping others, we tried our best to be at peace, trusting the order of the day, and affirming we would arrive at the perfect time.

When we finally arrived at the dealership, we were surprised to see that it wasn't busy at all. Then, upon entering, our salesperson greeted us stating he had just been discussing our concerns with his manager. After speaking for a bit, the manager joined us and listened attentively to our concerns. He assured us the car was a good choice, which we believed to be true, but still we wanted to have assurance. He then offered us a warranty that covered everything we were worried about at a considerable discount. He said it just so happened the CEO of that specific warranty company had stopped by the dealership only a few minutes before us, overheard the discussion, and wanted to extend this offer.

We were stunned to be on the receiving end of such an aligned gift. When we left, I told Shane, "Now, we have to celebrate this moment with a prayer of gratitude."

Our prayer was, "Thank you Holy Spirit for all the good you continue to bring into our lives. More of this please. We are listening." What should be noted, is that it truly doesn't matter what words you use in prayer. They should simply be your own.

Prayers of gratitude are especially important to vocalize because, often, when we receive a great accomplishment or blessing, our negative bias can manifest as self-sufficiency. We may default to believing that our prosperity happened solely through our own efforts. However, this could not be further from the truth. As my good friend and mentor Black Crow put it, "Manifestation cannot happen without the help of our ancestors. The help of spirit is always at the root of manifestation."

Because of my continued commitment, Holy instances like these are no longer rare for me. I have experienced windfalls of wealth unexpectedly at the exact time it was needed. I've been sought out to contribute to highly fulfilling projects that I could never have foreseen. I've honed my ability to listen intently, nurture loving connections, and tap into a gratitude so profound it moves me to tears and leaves my skin tingling, even amidst the uncertainty of life's twists and turns.

But it's not just the grand gestures that fill me with awe. It's the seemingly insignificant moments as well —the kind gesture of a stranger helping when my hands are full, a sincere compliment, instances of infectious laughter shared with my children, my husband's smile, endless green lights and up front parking spaces, the simple joy of providing nourishing meals, the grounding sensation of my feet connecting with the earth, the comfort of wrapping my arms around my loved ones or taking care of everyday tasks like washing dishes, paying bills, and tending a healing fire.

As a parent, I've also found prayer to be especially impactful in my growth as a mother. Prayer has a powerful nature of offering redemption for perceived mistakes and errors, transmuting them into guilt free experiences.

Prayer has offered me restoration when I have felt lost or at fault for tumultuous times within our family dynamic. During my early years as a mother, for instance, I often found the emotions of my children to be deeply triggering to me. I would internalize them as a reflection of who I am rather than seeing those emotions as part of my children's human experience, navigating this world in their own way. This was especially true regarding the emotion of anger.

In my childhood, anger was prevalent, but expression was stifled. Thus, in my adult life, anger used to trigger deep emotions within me. I would react defensively and even scold my children, urging them to shift their focus to gratitude instead —an impulse that aligns with toxic positivity, which is an unhealthy ideology advocating the suppression of perceived negative emotions. As well-intentioned as I was during those times, I have recognized it to be an unhealthy habit and I am glad I see that today.

A significant teaching moment for me occurred one morning when my son, Jack, woke up in a terrible and angry mood. He was searching through the cereal cabinet when my younger son, Roan, approached him to grab a box of cereal for himself. Feeling intruded upon, Jack reacted angrily by shoving the box at Roan. Roan, naturally upset, pushed Jack back. Jack then turned to physically retaliate but stopped himself. Caught off guard by this exchange, I immediately reacted harshly toward Jack. I raised my voice and scolded him, saying he shouldn't have done that and what was he thinking, before moving to comfort Roan.

The ride to school that day was very quiet. After dropping off both children, I broke down crying, overcome by the emotions of the morning. I felt guilty for reacting to the situation. Even though most people would agree that it wasn't right for anger to be directed toward Roan in that manner, the way in which I handled the situation left it closed to further investigation and I didn't want that as a mother. As a mother, I want to be someone who can listen with love, compassion, and without judgment.

On the drive home, I began my request for guidance. "Help me," I said. "Help me to see more clearly how to nurture in these moments. Help me to be available and to not react, but to see this as you would see the situation. Holy and loving spirit, ancestors, come into all my moments and show me how to do this as you would because I don't know what any of this means and I don't know what I'm doing."

It wasn't but a few moments later that I was given a vision of the same situation unfolding, but my part in it was different. Through my mind's eye, instead of reacting, I could see myself kneeling before each of my boys. With kindness and compassion, I said to them, "Hey, what's going on? That was a lot. Are you okay? Jack, are you okay? You seem frustrated and angry. Roan, are you okay? That must have hurt your feelings. Let's take a second to understand what just happened."

Even though I couldn't go back into the past to fix or redo the situation, this Holy Instant provided me with a new understanding of a loving connection I had never experienced in my young life. I was filled with hope and excitement for the opportunity to implement it in our lives. This type of realization is what it means to have a quantum leap. A quantum leap is a form of manifestation that occurs when you experience a radical shift in your mental understanding of life events. The result is a vibrational transformation that is aligned with the reality you want to achieve in your life. Prayer is a great tool for quantum leap visioning.

Through The Law of Celebration, I have learned that I can have joy in every moment, even those that I have considered failing moments. There was a time, I would spiral out with regret and guilt because of what others thought of me, a decision I made, or the way in which I behaved. I would sit with the energy of failure, sometimes for days. Sometimes for months and years, I would carry the cross of condemnation on my back, as I did when I carried the guilt of my assault or having experienced depression after the birth of my youngest son, Roan. What I now understand to be true, is that as we unfold, every "failed" moment offers an opportunity of transcendence, if we are willing to put down the cross and ask for the door to open.

I can't express enough how much this understanding has elevated my awareness regarding perceptions of success and failure. A notable aspect of double-mindedness is going through life labeling experiences as a success or a failure. However, these words are related to the outcome, which exists in the future. Since we don't actually know what the future holds, we are unqualified to place either of those labels on our experiences.

In A Course in Miracles, there is a passage called The Happy Dream. It says:

"Prepare you now for the undoing of what never was. If you already understood the difference between truth and illusion, the Atonement would have no meaning. The holy instant, the holy relationship, the Holy Spirit's teaching, and all the means by which salvation is accomplished, would have no purpose. For they are all but aspects of the plan to change your dreams of fear to happy dreams, from which you wake easily to knowledge.

Put yourself not in charge of this, for you cannot distinguish between advance and retreat. Some of your greatest advances you have judged as failures, and some of your deepest retreats you have evaluated as success.

Never approach the holy instant after you have tried to remove all fear and hatred from your mind. That is its function. Never attempt to overlook your guilt before you ask the Holy Spirit's help. That is His function. Your part is only to offer Him a little willingness to let Him remove all fear and hatred, and to be forgiven."

In other words, do not make yourself responsible for determining what is a failure and what is a success. Instead, allow communion with the Holy Spirit, The Universe, the Great Creator - whatever that is for you – and your ancestors to aid in transforming fear into happiness. Abstain from categorizing life events as successes or failures because this discernment is beyond the capacity of human understanding, therefore, it is not yours to make. Instead, maintain your sacred relationship by extending grace to yourself, expressing gratitude in moments of joy and celebrate forthcoming guidance in moments of grief and pain. In this way, you will maintain continuous atonement, which means repair, oneness, and unity with God Mind, in your venture toward the enduring bliss of stillness.

CHAPTER 9

The Law of Nonresistance

I AM resilient, graceful, and empowered as I face life's challenges with reverence and poise, experiencing the abundant flow of life with ease and effortlessness.

There is a Persian proverb that says, "He who wants the rose must respect the thorn." To me, this saying beautifully conveys that to experience life's beauty, we must also revere adversity. This applies to our life circumstances, as well as the journey of others. The Law of Non-Resistance embraces this wisdom, understanding that even when faced with uncontrollable situations and incompatible people, we can remain in the flow of universal supply through reverence and poise, which means to extend honor and respect to all of life with steadiness, balance, and composure.

Regarding circumstances in life, The Law of Nonresistance reminds us to be flexible in our thoughts and open to various, unseen solutions. Rather than anchoring ourselves to rigid expectations, this law invites us to trust our inherent knowing and the mysterious nature of the universe, of which we are a part. To fully embrace this law, rather than complaining or judging events as bad, we are encouraged to encounter each moment detached from a specific outcome, yet convinced that everything is working out in our favor.

It is important to recognize the practice of nonresistance does not imply numbness to adverse experiences. Rather, it involves honoring grief with acknowledgement and embracing challenges as integral parts of life, essential for cultivating resilience and realigning with an empowered sense of self.

The word "grief" is most often associated with loss, echoing its 13th-century interpretation, which signifies deep sorrow or anguish. However, its origin traces back to the Latin *gravis*, meaning "heavy" or "weighty," a concept closely linked to the Proto-Indo-European root *gwerə-*, also signifying heaviness or weight.

In the context of nonresistance, honoring grief in everyday life involves recognizing grief in two ways. The first, is by understanding that obstacles are part of life. When a difficulty presents itself, it is of course, completely natural to feel the burden of it, and it is also possible and valid to believe once your inner world is aligned, you can overcome the challenge.

Whether the hurdle in your way dissipates completely, or whether it is unmovable and unchangeable in every way, is irrelevant, all challenges present opportunities for inner growth.

Instead of resisting or being threatened by it, the way we "move mountains" is not so much about changing conditions as it is about changing ourselves. First by giving ourselves permission to express, experience, or at the very least acknowledge the burden. This approach not only honors our emotional responses but also serves as an antidote for energetic stagnation and spiritual growth, helping us to transform our reaction to the mountain standing in our way into a source of strength. By embracing weighty circumstances in this way, you become an observer to your emotional landscape and cultivate resilience in the face of life's challenges.

One of my favorite authors and spiritual teachers, the great Maya Angelou said, "I can be changed by what happens to me. But I refuse to be reduced by it."

I agree that life events do change us and how they change us is a choice. If we choose to resist, we will always consider ourselves victims of circumstance, in one way or another, but if we allow ourselves to trust that we are powerful beings in every way, then our subconscious minds will forever be resolving to expand our potential.

Maya Angelou was a woman who encountered many difficulties and traumatic events in her life and one of her most popular poems is, "Still, I Rise", a beautiful testament to the way in which we can overcome anything before us.

Another author I stumbled upon when I first began writing this book was Etty Hillesum, who tragically died in an Auschwitz concentration camp. Her book, *An Interrupted Life*, a collection of her diary entries, had a profound impact on me. Despite her imprisonment, she experienced continuous moments of awakening until her very last breath. In her writings, she speaks of God as an indwelling power residing within every person and in every moment, even the tragic moments she was experiencing, rather than as an external figure.

Hillesum's words are rich with spiritual wisdom as she chooses to see beauty amidst the tragedy unfolding before her eyes. She writes, "I really see no other solution than to turn inwards and to root out all the rottenness there. I no longer believe that we can change anything in the world until we first change ourselves. And that seems to me the only lesson to be learned."

Regarding the balance of life, Hillesum exemplifies acceptance, poise, and resilience. She states, "Everywhere things are both very good and very bad at the same time. The two are in balance, everywhere and always. I never have the feeling that I have got to make the best of things; everything is fine just as it is. Every situation, however miserable, is complete in itself and contains the good as well as the bad."

Throughout her writings, there is continued acknowledgement of the grief she is experiencing, and yet her outlook resembles Thich Nhat Hahn's philosophy of cultivating happiness by learning to suffer well and through that approach, she rises.

Grief as it relates to nonresistance, is helpful when navigating personal relationships, interactions with others, and fostering the capacity to let yourself accept all the feelings that come with especially triggering life events, because it does not serve us to breeze over them. Acknowledging deeper grief is how we cleanse and purify the energy of our minds and hearts.

The Law of Nonresistance is the ultimate surrender. It embodies aspects of co-creation that aligns with the understanding that you and the universe form a powerful majority. When you are grounded in faith and willing to be unthreatened by emotions of grief or burden —remaining open, trusting, curious, and considerate, despite appearances— you will find that there is no challenge large enough to defeat your inner world.

This Law can be applied in two ways. The first involves approaching current life situations with steadiness and composure. The second involves honoring the journey of every individual, including your own.

Let Spirit Have Its Way With You

Regarding life's challenges, we sometimes find ourselves stuck in downward spirals, trying to change the unchangeable, or wondering why we encounter stressful circumstances in the first place. We ruminate on why we aren't further along in life, believing that things should be different or that we should be doing more. These thoughts create barriers to our well-being by fostering resistance to the present moment. The solution, as an elder once expressed to me, is to "let spirit have its way with you."

Through this wisdom, I've come to understand that asking for circumstances to be different is ineffective because we are given free will. Free will implies that we are all on an individual path of personal choices, creating effects that ripple outward. Our reality is a mirror of our inner world. The universe, or God, is not an outer being that can be called upon to provide comforting feelings or simply remove hindrances, whether or not they were created by our actions. God is an inherent energy of love that grants us opportunities to seek or ask and develop the qualities needed to create what we desire.

I recently spoke with a new mother who was experiencing anxiety while caring for her newborn baby. She shared with me that her thoughts were consumed by body image concerns and a feeling that she needed to do more. This saddened me deeply because I recognize these thoughts are rooted in the loss of communal support and societal expectations—the belief that after having a baby, everything should return to "normal." In reality, there is no fixed "normal". Historically, our lineage included a village; we were never meant to navigate the path of parenthood alone. Thus, experiencing anxiety and depression is a very real occurrence for many women during these times, as it reflects our soul's yearning for connection and support.

I was able to relate to the anxiety and depression she was experiencing because I experienced it too. During my days as a new mother, I often wished that time would just stop because I was so overwhelmed. I didn't know how to navigate between the many obligations that *needed* my attention. I had thoughts of wishing my son had been born at a different time—a time when I had more of my business life together and wasn't caring for other family members, so that I could give him more attention.

It took me a year and a half of living in a depressive fog of anger and resentment toward the conditions of my life before I began to accept my life as it was. Rather than seeking to change it, I started asking for qualities of patience, peace, and wisdom that I could integrate into my life, helping me to become the version I desired for myself as a mother.

I'd like to say it was instant, but truth be told, my transformation was a gradual process of remembering to observe heavy emotions that lingered from my mistakes and hurdles I faced rather than resisting or pushing past them. It also required a willingness to maintain constant communication with Higher Truth, incorporating previous Laws of Stillness as I was directed.

Nonresistance meant learning to surrender activities fueled by low vibrational energy to create space for spirit's guidance. Instead of attaching meaning to the abrasive urgency of laundry, dishes, business affairs, and hardships as they arose, I taught myself to remain poised when circumstances weighed heavy on my mind and seek discernment, rather than rushing into action. In this way, I learned to address the many aspects of my life in their own time.

This shift allowed me to prioritize the well-being of myself and my family, fulfilling my desire to nurture our overall health and happiness first. Followed by clarity regarding business matters and other obligations. As I leaned into the desire for balance and remained open to receiving my next ordered step, I witnessed the natural transition of activities.

This is where the Law of Nonresistance intertwines further with Co-Creation, particularly the concept of spiritual time because it acknowledges that all aspects of life requiring attention are channels that must be attended to with poise. The present day definition of poise is composure, grace, and elegant bearing in a person, a description I especially love. Poise is further derived from the archaic definition, which means balance.

What I have learned is that when low vibrational energy is the fuel behind my present moment activity, it is because I am unbalanced in what I'm giving my attention to. Therefore, the rebel act of letting spirit have its way with me is to stop pursuing that activity momentarily and rest, awaiting guidance of the gentle whisper.

This understanding was at the root of every story I've shared in this book. It was present in the interaction I had with my son after attending Arun Ghandi's talk, lying on the floor of my office, the time I cleaned out my garage, my choice to forgive my mother by the fire. These aligned actions were a surrender to the present moment, letting spirit have its way with me, rather than imposing my will to continue on as I had planned. In turn, leading me to create balance in the many channels that serve my abundance.

Channels are pathways connected to your prosperity. It is important to recognize each channel in your life, so that you can realize when you are unbalanced and seek discernment.

To help understand this concept, picture yourself at the center of a circle, with rays of light extending outward from you. Each ray symbolizes a channel for the flow of abundance. While many people perceive their jobs or business affairs as the primary channels of abundance, the truth is that the ultimate source of everything in your life, including prosperity, is the energy of love within you—the essence of God, your ancestors, The Universe.

Everything you possess originates from this source. Therefore, the channels in your life encompass not only your work but also your hobbies, physical activities, relationships with your children, friends, and family, your travels, and especially your gifts. Every enjoyable aspect of your life serves as a channel. Giving attention to these channels when you are guided to, as the energy dictates, is the rebel act in that present moment that will open you to elevated consciousness through nonresistance.

Some may find the illustration of channels perplexing, questioning how one could possibly receive financial prosperity by being present with their children, spending time with friends, or a passion project, especially when work has presented so many tasks. The answer lies in understanding that abundance is not confined to a singular form. While it certainly includes material wealth, it extends far beyond, encompassing opportunities, connections, relationships, well-being, health, inner peace, and fulfillment. These forms of prosperity are progressive qualities that may not manifest immediately but as they are nurtured, blossom in the future through the attention we give.

Our gifts, including talents passed through our lineage and our children, represent especially potent channels of abundance. When nurtured with love and care, they reciprocate with a place to call home, boundless affection and they bring forth countless opportunities into our lives. Though it may sometimes feel that children are distractions to our abundance, that is an illusion of the past we must heal. Children encapsulate an effortless connection to God from the very instance of their birth and offer invaluable wisdom when given the opportunity to exercise their inner knowing.

As a parent, I've learned to practice nonresistance to the unique ways my children express themselves, which includes accepting their temperaments, as well as their intuitive nudges, rather than imposing my will upon them. This is a very difficult task and one I am still working on. A prayer I use to help me accept challenging moments rather than immediately acting on my impulse to insert my will comes from A Course in Miracles. It is simply, "Decide for me", which upon asking, offers me conscious space within my mind to better hear the whisper of aligned action.

The passage reads:

Say to the Holy Spirit only, "Decide for me," and it is done. For His decisions are reflections of what God knows about you, and in this light, error of any kind becomes impossible. Why would you struggle so frantically to anticipate all you cannot know, when all knowledge lies behind every decision the Holy Spirit makes for you?

To me, this serves as a reminder that while we strive to make things happen to suit our own needs, there is so much we do not know. By imposing our will upon a situation or person based on our perception of right or wrong, we are only resisting the natural unfoldment of the moment. Furthermore, we are interfering with the balance of the universe's self-organizing nature through each of us as we interact with one another. It is a delicate dance of trust and respect, acknowledging that every moment is as it should be.

I remember a time when my oldest son Jack, a complete water baby, insisted on swimming in mountain stream water after hiking on a cold fall day. His lips were turning blue, yet he insisted on staying in longer. I didn't want to engage in a battle of wills, so despite my worry, I said "10 more minutes" aloud, but in my head and heart, I whispered, "Decide for me." Less than a minute later, he came back to us, ready for a towel, on the timeline determined by his inner knowing.

This experience highlighted for me the importance of understanding that spiritual timing is alive and active in every moment, when I maintain poise.

Regardless of what adversities are present, my inner world thrives, and I notice that life transitions naturally, much like water flowing effortlessly around stones blocking the way. Irrespective of the situation at hand, there is no real need for force or struggle.

This principle applies to every circumstance in our lives. As a business owner and marketing professional, I once experienced a month where I lost two large clients, significantly decreasing my commission. There was a time when I would have absolutely entered into a downward spiral, but because I was already well on my way practicing the Laws in this book, I was able to view the situation as an observer. I accepted it as something that was right for them since it was their choice to discontinue our partnership, and therefore, in this moment it must also be right for me.

Initially, I felt pangs of anxiety, but acknowledging those emotions, remembering that I am supported in all ways as a co-creator of my world, and keeping channels open by forgiving them, I handled their departure with grace and moved through the grief quickly. On the other side of this challenge, I found three new clients to take their place and down the road both of the clients that had not renewed reentered a partnership with me. Reflecting on previous experiences, I know that without the practice of these Laws, I would have been stuck in a downward spiral for days, unable to quickly receive the prosperity that always comes when one door closes.

Change is inevitable in life, but one constant is that when you consider the balance of the universe, any void you experience will always be filled. Whether you intentionally release something, as discussed in The Law of Creating Space, or a substantial change occurs unexpectedly, the vacuum formed will be filled with what is meant for you. This natural equilibrium ensures that every empty space is replaced by something aligned with your highest good.

Therefore, it is important to not allow sensations of urgency or thoughts of *needing* something to happen, to direct your movement. By remaining nonresistant to grief, allowing it to naturally dissipate, you can trust that whatever you pursue, you will be provided with everything necessary and guided effortlessly when redirection is needed.

In ancient Chinese philosophy, nonresistance is often illustrated through the nature of water. In ancient Taoism, Chinese Zen Buddhism, and Confucianism (including Neo-Confucianism), the flowing nature of water carries qualities such as power, creativity, human nature, nurturance, peace, wisdom, and enlightenment. Water's versatile nature and imagery guides soul seekers to understand themselves, perceive life, and learn how to live in a way that honors their spiritual unfoldment. I find this wisdom especially meaningful considering our bodies are 70% water.

Laozi said, "The best man is like water. Water is good; it benefits all things and does not compete with them. It dwells in lowly places that all disdain. This is why it is so near Tao." This saying emphasizes that water, regardless of its circumstances, does not resist its reality or seek to change its surrounding nature; it finds its place in the present moment.

Another insight provided by this master teacher states, "There is nothing stronger and weaker than water, yet there is nothing better for attacking hard and strong things. For this reason, there is no substitute for it." This means that although water may seem soft or invisible at times, it is a cumulative force that can wear away obstructions in its path.

In response to a student's question, another Zen master replied, "You are like all those who, while immersed in the ocean, extend their hands crying for water." This suggests there is never a need to grasp, you are already surrounded by all that you need at this moment.

The true practice of aligning with nonresistance is to be an observer to the physical sensations of urgency, recognizing them to be manifestations of the subconscious mind, which is only focused on survival. It is also the body not being accustomed to the sensations of waiting for order through peace and rest. Since the spiritual experience of elevating consciousness occurs on a plane with no immediate or visible signs of progress, we must acclimate our physical senses with gracious acceptance of the mystery that exists within the present moment, even when our bodies are flooded with urgency. We make the choice to intentionally surrender to the flowing nature of nonresistance, a powerful force that fosters freedom.

In the Greek analysis of Romans 12:1-2, it says, "Therefore, brothers, by the mercies of God, I urge you to present your bodies as a living sacrifice, holy and pleasing to God; this is your spiritual worship. And do not be conformed to this world, but be transformed by the renewing of your mind, that you may prove what the will of God is, that which is good and acceptable and perfect."

The instruction to present your body as a living sacrifice is a call to surrender the physical senses driven by worldly obligations. This wisdom directs us to not allow the urgency of outer circumstances to guide our actions. Do not conform to this world means do not let the world, as it has influenced your lens of right and wrong, dictate what is yours to do in this moment or convince you of your rightful place. You have a unique expression that can only be found in communion with Higher Consciousness.

Another teaching in A Course in Miracles that mirrors this idea is the principle of *I need do nothing*. It explains:

I need do nothing is a statement of allegiance, a truly undivided loyalty. Believe it for just one instant, and you will accomplish more than is given to a century of contemplation, or of struggle against temptation.

Emphasizing the time saving qualities of having a holy relationship, it further says:

Now you need but to remember you need do nothing. It would be far more profitable now merely to concentrate on this than to consider what you should do. When peace comes at last to those who wrestle with temptation and fight against the giving in to sin; when the light comes at last into the mind

166

given to contemplation; or when the goal is finally achieved by anyone, it always comes with just one happy realization; I need do nothing.

This passage reminds me of all the times I have worried about problems beyond my control until I reached my breaking point and finally stopped resisting. Then in the moments that follow, I find that all the worry was for nothing. When the solution is realized, it's never by my own doing.

It is important that I add, the use of the word "sin" in the passage above, or any Biblical passage for that matter, does not refer to original evil as it does in organized religion. Instead, it is drawn from the original Hebrew meaning of 'missing the mark.' In this context, it signifies making a mistake, straying from the path of one-mindedness, or becoming unaligned with your spiritual intentions, which is never permanent or punishable. The opposite, actually. To realize you have "missed the mark" offers opportunities for revelation and healing.

As the passage continues in A Course in Miracles, *to do something* involves the body, but if you recognize you *need do nothing*, you can withdraw the body's sense of urgency from your mind. In doing this, you are no longer vulnerable to the past or future outcome and time becomes irrelevant. To do nothing, it says is to rest, and make a place within you where the activity of the body ceases to demand attention. In this space, you will be "directed how to use the body sinlessly."

In other words, you will be directed to use the body in aligned action. "I need do nothing" is a surrender

167

to universal communion and the expansiveness of spiritual time, rather than your own will.

Honor the Journey of Others

When practicing nonresistance in relationships, stillness is harnessed through honoring the journey of others, regardless of how they have treated us or the harm they have caused themselves. When we embody The Law of Nonresistance, we recognize that every person is walking a unique path of the soul. They, too, have memories resurfacing, traumas they seek to heal, passions, dreams, and fears. At the core of it all, we are all trying our best to discover our place in this ever-changing world.

When it comes to relationships, especially with close family members, embracing this law has been the most challenging for me, and I have experienced a lot of anguish arising from being emotionally and mentally uncared for throughout my young life. Even through experiences of being assaulted, losing a baby, and enduring the grief of postpartum depression I have not had close family members that I could easily confide in or who could hold space for my pain, which has always weighed heavily on me.

Early in life, as the oldest sibling in a single parent household, I became the go-to person for family members. I always said "yes," believing it was my role to do so. Over time, I noticed that despite giving so much of myself, that same level of energy was not often reciprocated. Instead, I have been blamed, criticized, and guilted for not doing more. These experiences influenced a tendency within myself to feel overly responsible for circumstances outside of my realm of control and guilt for not being able to meet the expectations of others.

When it came time for me to care for my own family, I had to teach myself that it was not just okay, but necessary, as a spiritual being, to focus my love and attention on what truly fulfills my soul. Though my venture hasn't been perfect, I am learning to release anything that doesn't align with this standard of self-love. This involves recognizing which relationships uplift me and which ones drain my energy by demanding that I give out of obligation— whether that be through financial support, enduring emotional dumping, or being present in environments filled with low-frequency energy.

The challenge I faced during my early years, is that I understood to some extent the idea of nonresistance, but I didn't know how to apply it.   I thought nonresistance meant to be passive with requests made of me or the ill treatment I received from others. Even when deep feelings of sadness, resentment, bitterness, and anger were leaking into other aspects of my life, my trauma response was to blame myself. I thought I wasn't compassionate or strong enough in spirit.   Really, the issue was that I was applying nonresistance to requests being made of me, while resisting my unfoldment by suppressing grief and continuing to give of myself even when physical, mental, and spiritual discomfort was present.   This was especially true regarding close relatives, because after all, "family is family".

A great influence in my understanding of this aspect of The Law of Nonresistance came from author and New Thought teacher Myrtle Fillmore. In her book Healing Letters, she writes, "You have been made to feel that nonresistance, and righteousness, and Christianity, and loving service are all passive. You have allowed your personal ideas of love and good will to make you too sympathetic and inclined to give, without seeking and asking for wisdom and good judgment to direct you."

Fillmore further explains that while it is virtuous to always be willing to help others, we must ensure that we are actually helping them rather than hindering their unfoldment by doing for them what they are capable of achieving themselves - mostly through communion with the same Holy power that exists within us and within them.

She also elaborates that in the same way we believe in two powers, or experience double-mindedness, in our own affairs, we similarly direct our mental power toward others. "In the same breath," she says, "You say that he has been upheld by the Spirit these months *and* that you feel he cannot stand the strain much longer!" Meaning we pray for others while simultaneously pitying them or seeing them as incapable of rising from the ashes as they access their own inner wisdom.

A significant shift in my understanding of stillness, particularly regarding nonresistance in relationships, occurred after separate interactions with two individuals very close to me who have faced many challenges, including addiction. Our relationships have long been strained, and we've rarely seen eye to eye. Over the years and for a long time, I responded passively to harsh words, blame, and criticism directed at me, believing that was the compassionate and nonresistant thing to do.

One day, after getting off a call that ended yet again with hurtful words and abrupt disconnection, I found myself feeling distraught. An exercise I did at that time when these incidents happened was to enter into a meditation in which I imagined these individuals surrounded by light and I would envision myself reaching out to hug them. This was my way of giving love from a distance.

On this day, I entered the practice as I normally did, creating an image of these individuals, happy and healthy. However, as I began to reach my arms out to embrace them, in my mind's eye, my arms were instead pulled into a prayer position at my heart before moving to touch my third eye, as I bowed to them. I was then given an image of them in their part of the world and me in my part of the world each surrounded by light. As always, I was filled with awe from this vision, that I had not consciously produced, and the way in which it provided me with such profound guidance.

The action of palms meeting is a sacred hand gesture found throughout the world. In Christianity and Catholicism it symbolizes prayer, a request or expression of gratitude toward God. I, however, found myself considering it in terms of Indian spirituality and what is found throughout Asia, where this position is named by the Sanskrit word Añjali and symbolizes respect and reverence. The word Añjali is derived from anj, which means to honor and celebrate. The gesture of palms touching is called Mudra in Sanskrit, which means "seal". In most yoga practices, the gesture of Añjali Mudra, is a position of holding prayer hands to the heart chakra, with thumbs touching the sternum. This position has the same meaning as the Sanskrit greeting Namaste, which means, "I bow to the divinity within you, from the divinity within me."

I found it to be beautiful that my prayer hands did not just offer Namaste to this individual, they moved upward to touch the space between my eyebrows, which is where the third eye chakra is located. The third eye is the place of inner vision and Higher Consciousness. The touching of the space between our eyebrows is significant in connecting the two hemispheres of our brain, the left being the side of reason and the right being the side of emotion and spirituality. It is also identified as a connecting point to the pineal gland, which is known as a center of ethereal energy. When the third eye, or pineal gland, is activated, a great spiritual clarity is gained, as is the ability to access our super consciousness mind that sees beyond physical reality.

I realized that while my intentions were good in visualizing an embrace in previous meditative moments, there was also an element of pity because I couldn't do more for these individuals. This new vision, however, empowered me to surrender both their path and my own to God, embracing nonresistance and resisting judgement regarding the many ways our unique journeys are bound to weave and turn as we make our way. Añjali Mudra at my heart center guided me to celebrate their light and offer respect to their passage through life. Añjali Mudra at my third eye reminded me that I am not witness to the unseen realm of possibility swirling around them and just as I am divinely connected, so are they.

I believe that when it comes to others, we often forget they too have access to God, and we mistakenly assume responsibility for guiding them through their circumstances. Instead of waiting for heavenly wisdom, we can be overtaken by a sense of obligation, pushing through our emotions rather than seeking transcendence through a higher understanding. In doing so, we not only disrupt the journey of others but our own as well.

The responsibility we have regarding others is the same as it is in every other situation - to wait for the order of our steps to be revealed, which is to align with a consciousness of stillness.

When it comes to offering support to others, I now ask, "What is mine to do here?" and I wait, going about my day, until a solution I am at ease with is presented. Sometimes nothing comes up, and I've learned to trust the peace that accompanies that silence. In these instances, I recognize my responsibility is to simply praise and maintain reverence for the way of others while honoring my own, which means maintaining boundaries in interactions that affect my vibrational wellbeing.

Other times, a solution does present itself, and when it does, it is always aligned with the beat of my heart and when accepted by the other person ends up being the perfect solution. Sometimes, the solution that works for me does not work for the other person. In those situations, I've learned it is because they are not ready or willing to receive what I can give, and I have to accept that. This process has helped me establish boundaries in a life affirming way. Rather than cutting people off, I stay grounded in what is true for me. If, at some point, that truth also works for them, there will always be a door where we can meet.

All in all, this is a perspective of accepting people as they are and then deciding if that aligns with where you are and what you desire for your life. A quote from spiritual teacher and Reverend Dr. Iyanla Vanzant resonates with this idea. She says, "You have to meet people where they are, and sometimes you have to leave them there."

This has been another valuable lesson for me. I now picture our interconnectedness as walking on the same path toward individual fulfillment. Sometimes, we walk together for a while, but then one of us may stop and sit, take a different path, or rush ahead. The universal mystery is always present because we never know if we will reunite or go our separate ways. Either way, I can have deep respect for you, wishing you all the best, and I hope you'll do the same for me.

Of course, often this is easier said than done, as a great deal of grief can arise as we relinquish control, accepting others as they are and the paths they choose. It's important to acknowledge this heaviness. Especially when pursuing a path of spiritual unfoldment, grief becomes a valuable tool for mourning aspects of life that don't turn out as we had hoped.

Whether it's simply acknowledging the distress from recent interactions or experiencing an emotional release of compounded pain, embracing grief with nonresistance opens us to the opportunity of rediscovering forgotten parts of ourselves and cultivating compassion for others. Grief can be expressed in many ways, such as breathing through emotional energy, deep sobbing, journaling, or speaking aloud the distress you're feeling in the moment, along with any regrets about situations or relationships. Many of us have been taught to view grief as a weakness or to reserve it for major losses and funerals, however, grief is a powerful force. On the other side of grief is the remembrance of who we've been, what we've been through, and the unlimited possibilities of who we are becoming.

In the Indigenous practices of Mesoamerican Shamanism, particularly among the earliest civilizations of the Mexica and Yucatán Mayan people, beautiful traditions of using the spoken word to express grief were very common. This practice was not only used ceremonially for coming of age rites, but also encouraged as a daily activity. Today, it is referred to as a platica or a heart talk. In ancient codices, images of breath and spoken words are depicted as offerings given in exchange for celestial help. During the Spanish conquest of the Yucatán, Friar Diego de

Landa labeled this practice as a form of baptism after destroying as many ancient texts as he could find. However, these traditions were far deeper than merely washing away errors. The platica was a way of achieving deep connection, renewal, and keeping oneself spiritually free.

In Peru, similar practices to the Mesoamerican "platica" or heart talk can be found among various Indigenous groups. Among the Quechua people, who are the largest indigenous group in Peru, traditional ceremonies and communal gatherings often serve as opportunities for emotional expression and collective healing. These gatherings are deeply rooted in the Andean worldview, which emphasizes a close relationship with nature and the cosmos. Other Indigenous groups include elements of storytelling, allowing individuals to share their grief and receive support from their community. These practices, like the Mesoamerican "platica," emphasize the importance of the expression of emotions in maintaining psychological and spiritual well-being.

When I was eighteen, I had an experience akin to a "heart talk" upon returning from Texas to visit my family in Knoxville, TN. During this visit, I made a trip to the sacred land, where years prior, I was introduced to Native American practices and participated in my first sweat lodge. Despite my brief stay in town, I eagerly said "yes" to an event taking place during my visit, arriving ready to immerse myself in whatever unfolded.

This event turned out to be far more impactful than I could have imagined. It was a three-day session where we sat in a circle each day from morning to evening, sharing the spoken word of accumulated grief residing in our inner worlds. We weren't allowed to write or journal; instead, we sat in the presence of each other, strangers at that time, sharing what weighed heavily on our hearts and minds. It was an experience of vulnerability and letting go of compounded grief that has since become a cherished part of my story.

In Chapter six, I shared about a morning I spent by the fire, ruminating on an exchange concerning my mother. What I didn't share is that I entered a period of deep despair that day. In the weeks that followed, I mourned both the reality of our connection and the unmet expectations I'd been carrying. Allowing myself to grieve led me to a simple truth: she is who she is. Finding peace meant giving her a new name, accepting her as she is, and letting go of expectations that were beyond my control.

As part of my healing process, I engaged in several platicas speaking aloud what I was feeling, giving what I regretted to the fire, and welcoming all the emotions that arose within me, no longer concerned whether it was right or wrong to feel them. If I'm being honest, I simply let myself fall apart. I eventually realized that beyond the interaction between my mother and I, I was also undergoing an intense purge of accumulated pain from various unfortunate past events. As days and weeks passed, I allowed spirit to guide me through this deep despair, and on the other side of that grief I found restoration. I was profoundly empowered by this process. Not only did I foster empathy for my mother and appreciation for our shared history, but I found it easier to remember the good times, which was especially meaningful for me.

To this day, I still get triggered from time to time, though nowhere near what I once did. The great lesson I've learned is that I must pay close attention to my emotional state, maintain grace, and welcome any emotions that arise. It is stillness in action to acknowledge all emotional energy. In doing so, I can better discern my authentic self from my mistakes and the actions of others.

It is helpful to remember The Law of Creating Space in any grief process by utilizing soul questions. Emotional energy is transformed when prompted by the intention of creating space for solution, not by dwelling in the heavy energy or in the question of "why me?". This is crucial to The Law of Nonresistance because "why me?" keeps energy stagnant. Instead acknowledge the thoughts and feelings of anxiety, sadness, frustration, unworthiness as an observer would. Then ask for help understanding the experience with curiosity and willingness.

Spirit is always available when we ask for guidance and are willing to embrace every part of who we are and what we are experiencing energetically in the moment.

Author and Psychologist Dr. Gabor Mate says, "Grief is not a disorder, a disease, or a sign of weakness. It is an emotional, physical, and spiritual necessity, the price you pay for love. The only cure for grief is to grieve."

Embracing grief is an act of self-love. Maintaining poise, being flexible with life's challenges that provoke anguish, and embracing these instances with openness, trust, and curiosity deepen your connection with the gentle whisper of your soul. Through this practice, you will discover that nothing can hinder what is meant for you from manifesting in your life.

The Law of Nonresistance exists as a reminder that you and the universe form a powerful majority. By recognizing yourself as a spiritual being navigating a human existence, the grace, resilience, and vulnerability you cultivate within have the potential to inspire positive change in the world around you. This essence is encapsulated in the principle of loving your neighbor as yourself. Regardless of circumstances or wrongdoings, embrace acceptance. Allow spirit to help you realize an awakened capacity for profound bliss that transcends earthly comprehension.

CHAPTER 10

The Light that is You

I AM a spiritual rebel on a path of unfolding my truest self. I now welcome the loving energy of life to guide me on my unique journey.

Achieving true and lasting inner stillness takes a rebellious commitment to honor your innate truth by shedding societal constructs that have shaped your self-perception and interactions with the world. This process involves embracing the unique journey of your soul, allowing grief to be acknowledged and be transformed by higher thoughts of Truth. Cultivating stillness means developing the ability to remain nonresistant to the various cycles and flows of life, the conditions of the world, and the personalities around you. Far beyond the mere absence of movement, stillness is a consciousness of order and rest, a harmonious balance between awaiting guidance and knowing when to act.

The Five Laws of Stillness have significantly influenced my life by validating the unique energy I carry from my personal history. They demonstrate that achieving sustainable peace of mind is not a one-size-fits-all process. Rather, it involves a continuous exploration of how past conditioning influences the present moment, approached with reverence and love rather than judgment.

These Laws guide us in deepening our connection with the vitality of life, leading us into blissful and abundant presence through our inherent creativity and worthiness.

While each law offers invaluable wisdom on its own, they are also interconnected, forming a cohesive and progressive path.

Positioned as the culmination of this spiritual undertaking, The Law of Nonresistance is the ultimate surrender. It teaches us to flow with the natural currents of life rather than struggle against them. Embodying this Law fortifies your spirit and aligns you more deeply with the organizing rhythm of the universe, keeping your energy in motion for continuous renewal and building resilience for life's challenges and difficult relationships. By embracing nonresistance, we learn to accept grief that arises from obstacles with poise, trusting that with inherent wisdom, we can overcome any challenge.

Fully connecting with The Law of Nonresistance, however, is only possible through practicing the preceding Laws, which naturally develop qualities of reverence and poise. As you become more aware of double-mindedness, release stagnant energy, welcome co-creation, and offer prayer and praise in instances of uncertainty and gratitude alike, it becomes nearly impossible to meet adversity without empathy or composure. The preceding Laws prime you for this very outcome. Overall, they serve as stepping stones, moving us from our attachment to the physical world into the superconscious realm.

For instance, The Law of Celebration is necessary to understand prior to The Law of Nonresistance because it introduces the concepts of praise and prayer. This trains our minds to positively rename troubling situations and people, deepening our ability to celebrate every moment, knowing we are always supported.

The Law of Co-Creation enhances our ability to celebrate by expanding our awareness and reminding us that we have never been alone in our endeavors. Despite societal conditioning, we are not meant to be all things, to all people, at all times. Each of us is a unique expression on a sacred adventure as co-creators, aligned with gifts unique to our souls and bestowed by a Higher Power. Universal guidance and collaboration are always within reach. Therefore, there is always reason to celebrate.

Furthermore, just as you cannot renovate a home without discarding worn-out furniture, you cannot effectively create if your mind is occupied with doubt and fear. Therefore, The Law of Co-Creation is only possible by realizing The Law of Creating Space. It is essential to release the physical, mental, and spiritual clutter you carry within to make room for growth and new beginnings.

Finally, it all begins with The Law of One-Mindedness, which helps us identify and understand our thought patterns, perceptions, and behaviors. As we enhance our awareness, we become skilled at recognizing thought energy and aligning it with Infinite Wisdom. This practice enables us to choose thoughts that serve our highest good and let go of those that do not, fostering a mindset that awakens potential.

Through the recognition of these Universal Laws, it is possible to find yourself living everyday life in stillness, allowing spirit to have its way with you.

Much more than a carved-out time in a specific place, stillness is a way of being that transforms the energy you carry in the present moment through order. First, by healing perceptions, then by providing revelation about who you've been, how you came to this moment, and the revised narrative you're here to create for your life and the world.

It is the act of a rebel to align with this outlook because it requires willingness to embrace the possibilities of unseen solutions, even when surrounding circumstances seem out of control. It is the aligned act of surrendering to indwelling Truth. The consciousness of stillness is a skill that has been shown to us throughout the eras by thought leaders and master teachers.

Martin Luther King Jr., was yet another example of someone whose presence manifested a movement.

With poise, love, and peace, he walked through crowds of people who hated him, steadfast carrying the message that was his to share. Looking at videos, without context, you might not even know that he was surrounded by a storm considering the peace he radiated and gifted to others by his very presence. I believe he too viewed his life as a series of ordered steps, divinely directed in each moment. I can only imagine the fearful emotions and thoughts that he had to presently transform so that he could move forward in love.

Just as Jesus, without willingness to stand in the space between his movements, King would have been carried by the impulsive energy to react or retreat amid the chaos, failing to leave the powerful impression that he did. Instead, every step he made was grounded in love and made with a clear intention to heal divisiveness among the people, which positively influenced many to take their place beside him. Martin Luther King Jr. once said, "One day we must come to see that peace is not merely a distant goal that we seek, but that it is a means by which we arrive at that goal. We must pursue peaceful ends through peaceful means."

Jesus, Martin Luther King Jr., and other master teachers from Mother Theresa, Laozi to Buddha, and those that came between and after, were all rebels of their time. They embodied a consciousness of stillness and shared that with others as they embarked on their individual paths. They understood stillness as a necessary surrender to access eternal guidance from within, regardless of what was happening around them. Their mission was to bring connection to a disconnected world, and they achieved this by cultivating such rest within themselves that they discovered how to find their place amid the chaos.

Most noteworthy is that each confesses, in their own words, that they are not the source of the miracles they deliver, but merely the vessel for a power greater than themselves working in and through them. A power that can be realized by every single person. Not only is it possible that you too can realize this power, but existing in stillness is your sacred right as a steward of the earth.

Our work at this time is to establish order in our being by waiting on divine guidance. As such, we invite the flow of what is ordained by heaven into our lives and extend the peace we cultivate into the world. Chief White Eagle, who is credited for enforcing change in Native American civil rights in response to the Ponca Trail of Tears said, "When you are in doubt, be still, and wait; when doubt no longer exists for you, then move forward with courage. So long as mists envelop you, be still; be still until the sunlight pours through and dispels the mists – as it surely will. Then act with courage."

This is a shift in consciousness we are being called to embody. It is the consciousness of our ancestors, exemplifying balance and flow between action and surrender. Most importantly, it is a consciousness of waiting in love for guidance until the sacred voice within calls us to move forward.

In that moment, stillness may manifest as lying on the floor with your breath as the only movement, locking eyes with your child as you listen deeply, or allowing yourself to grieve by the fire. Whatever calls to you through the energy of your being, in that present moment, that is your stillness in action. Even if what lies on the other side of that moment remains unclear, surrender yourself to the unseen and bear witness to the unfoldment of your soul.

My deepest desire is that these Laws serve you as they have served me, and that through them, you find the encouragement and permission to unfold your layers and unveil to the world the light that is you.

AFTERWORD

On September 27th, 2024, Hurricane Helene upended the lives of so many in Western North Carolina where I live. The storm brought destruction, leaving our communities reeling from the damage.

Before fully understanding the gravity of the storm, our family treated the first two nights as an adventure, almost like camping. We played games by candlelight, cooked on a propane stove, and waited for the power and cell service to return. But on the third day, I ventured out to get ice, and that's when reality struck. I took the only route out of our neighborhood and saw, for the first time, the extent of the damage—fallen trees, crushed homes, and other signs of destruction.

When I reached the main road, an endless line of cars stretched toward the only gas station with power. Not needing gas, I turned toward the grocery store instead. There, cars were parked on every patch of grass and spare inch of pavement, lines wound around the building, "cash-only" signs hung on doors, and people moved with confusion and panic.

Abandoning my plan to find ice, I turned back to head home but got caught in the deadlocked traffic I'd passed earlier. I tried side roads, but each one was blocked by fallen trees. My phone showed "S.O.S."—no navigation, no way to contact my husband, no clue what lay beyond the walls of my SUV. The fear and panic of being trapped gripped me in a way I had never felt before.

Eventually, I made it home by weaving through alleys, navigating around downed trees, and cutting through parking lots. Days later, as cell service was sporadically restored, I was able to see the devastation in places like Biltmore Village, Chimney Rock, Lake Lure, Swannanoa, Burnsville, Marshall, Hot Springs, Spruce Pine, among other surrounding areas, and it hit me—my feeling of being trapped was nothing compared to what others endured and this was a heartbreaking realization to swallow.

The morning that Helene hit, I had actually just completed my final read through of this book, but in the days that followed, I remained shaken and questioned whether releasing it was the right thing to do. How could I speak of stillness and inner peace, amid such suffering? Even though this book directly addresses fostering peace in the midst of a storm, I was in such disbelief at what had transpired.

As the weeks passed and our region found small ways to begin again, I assisted in a grief ceremony led by Black Crow. There, all who attended were given an opportunity to speak openly about the experience that had terrified them the most—without comparison or judgment. This act of self-love and vulnerability to grief brought me back to unwavering Truth.

And once again, *The Five Laws of Stillness* became my anchor during this time, grounding me in inner peace and helping me remember that, even in devastation, our good is not limited. Even as life events unfold in mystery, we remain forces of love, reflections of a Great Creator.

The Law of Creating Space was at work as I released what I no longer needed, offered to others, and forgave what had unfolded, allowing me to stay open to guidance. Co-creation was listening to the voice within directing me to be of service, checking in with people, raising funds, buying essential supplies, and delivering them to those in need. In practicing celebration, I prayed for our land and all people grappling with their losses, turning toward the beauty of falling leaves, trees, and the mountains that surround us. Nonresistance allowed me to welcome grief as it arrived in waves, adjusting to a new normal of bearing witness to others' sorrow through deeply personal stories—stories of lost heirlooms, children left parentless, homes destroyed, and towns erased.

I'm humbled and honored to be entrusted with these stories and grateful to share my own. In our fast-moving world, practicing these Laws has shown me that being truly present for this kind of connection is a rare and sacred art.

The aftermath of Helene further validated the powerful truths explored in this book—that stillness is not simply found in solitude or silence. True and lasting stillness is born from the decision to stay attuned to life, embracing the understanding that we are part of something greater, even when that something is painful or beyond our comprehension. Sometimes, stillness is found in death itself, in the transition back to God, back to the Earth—a truth that humbles and grounds me.

I hold the awareness that life is fragile, never guaranteed, and that we must live each moment fully, as vessels of love and service. Our purpose is not just to survive but to thrive through our connection with one another, helping, praying, and seeing beyond separation. This is how we create a future that honors both our dreams and our shared humanity.

The journey toward stillness, is one that calls us to honor and nurture our innermost self so that we can more easily unfold our layers to act with love, compassion, and empathy for one another. And in the quiet after the storm, we come to see that stillness, is a dynamic force, emerging not despite adversity, but because of it.

Western North Carolina will for years to come need and welcome your generosity. Please consider some of our local organizations as places to contribute. Here are a few that would welcome your support:

Unity of The Blue Ridge: unityofblueridge.org

Beloved Asheville: belovedasheville.com

Black Mountain Home for Children: blackmountainhome.org

Bounty & Soul: bounty&soul.org

GLOSSARY OF TERMS

Awakening Moment: *A profound realization or shift in awareness that dramatically changes how an individual perceives themselves, others, and the world around them. It is often a moment of clarity where deeper truths are revealed, leading to a heightened sense of consciousness, spiritual insight, or personal understanding. This moment can trigger significant personal transformation, guiding you toward a more authentic, purposeful, and connected way of living. An awakening moment is usually associated with the beginning of a spiritual journey or a significant leap in personal growth.*

Double-Mindedness: *A state of internal conflict where an individual simultaneously holds two contradictory beliefs, attitudes, or desires. This inner division can lead to indecision, inconsistency, and lack of focus. In a spiritual context, double-mindedness describes the struggle between higher spiritual truths and lower, ego-driven fears or doubts. It creates wavering faith and confusion, preventing full commitment to a spiritual path or purpose. This divided mindset can hinder personal growth and inner peace, making it challenging to achieve clarity and spiritual alignment. Overcoming double-mindedness involves harmonizing one's beliefs, intentions, and actions with The Highest Thought.*

Forgiveness: *The highest expression of love, a profound act that transcends mere forgetfulness. It is a conscious and intentional release of judgments, expectations, and perceived wrongdoings, allowing them to dissipate into the loving embrace of God. Through forgiveness, we choose to free both ourselves and others from the weight of past hurts, creating space for healing, compassion, and a deeper connection to the universal love that binds us all.*

God Mind: *A state of consciousness that embodies inner wisdom, love, and universal truth. It is often understood as the highest level of awareness or spiritual insight, where one aligns with the infinite intelligence and creative power of the universe. In this state, the individual transcends the limitations of the ego and human perception, accessing a deeper understanding of oneness, interconnectedness, and the Holy nature of all existence.*

Intuition: *The innate ability to access the foresight of universal wisdom that resides within every person, guiding us beyond logic and reasoning. It is the inner knowing that connects us to a deeper understanding, often revealing truths and insights that the conscious mind may not immediately recognize. Through intuition, we tap into the collective wisdom of the universe, allowing us to make decisions and perceive reality with a sense of clarity and alignment with our Highest Self.*

Soul Questions: *Inquiries designed to uncover the roots of emotional charges and foster a deeper connection with our inner wisdom. Unlike the question "Why me?"—which often perpetuates feelings of victimhood—soul questions invite us to shift our focus from blame to understanding, encouraging a life-affirming exploration of our spiritual quests. By asking soul questions, we open ourselves to the answers provided by Infinite Intelligence, which prompts us to recognize our role as channels of omnipotent solutions.*

Spiritual Time: *A sense of time that transcends the linear, clock-based concept we typically follow in daily life. It is experienced as a more fluid, expansive, and nonlinear dimension where past, present, and future are interconnected. In spiritual time, moments of insight, growth, and transformation unfold according to divine timing, aligning with the soul's purpose. This concept emphasizes that significant spiritual experiences and realizations occur when the soul is ready, rather than when the physical world dictates. Spiritual time is associated with the idea that everything happens for a reason and in its perfect time within the grand design of the universe.*

Synchronicity: *A spiritual concept that refers to meaningful coincidences or events that appear to be connected by more than just chance. These occurrences often seem to defy ordinary explanations and are perceived as signs or messages* from the universe, guiding individuals along their spiritual path. In a state of heightened awareness, synchronicity is the alignment of external events with an individual's internal state, reflecting a deeper connection between the mind, spirit, and the unfolding of divine order.

The Rebel Act: A spiritually and blissfully aligned action that resonates deeply with one's inner guidance or Higher Self, even when it defies logic or expectations based on external circumstances and inherited beliefs. It is an intuitive choice that prioritizes spiritual truth over conventional norms, challenging the status quo in a way that is true to one's spiritual path.

The Still Small Voice, AKA The Gentle Whisper: The subtle, yet profound communication delivered by Higher Consciousness that gently nudges us toward truth, wisdom, and alignment with our deepest values. Unlike the loud and demanding voices of the ego or external world, the Still Small Voice is calm, reassuring, and rooted in love, offering clarity and direction in a way that resonates with our innermost self.

The Highest Thought: The most elevated, pure, and spiritually aligned idea or intention one can hold. It represents a thought or insight that is in harmony with one's highest values, deepest truths, and revelatory understanding of universal principles. This thought transcends ordinary, ego-driven desires and is characterized by clarity, wisdom, and alignment with an elevated purpose or spiritual reality. Embracing The Highest Thought involves focusing on ideas that uplift and inspire, fostering personal and spiritual growth while contributing to the greater good.

Quantum Leap: A sudden, significant change or abrupt shift in consciousness, perspective, or life circumstances that propels an individual to a much greater level of understanding, awareness, or achievement. It is often seen as a breakthrough moment, where progress happens rapidly, bypassing the gradual steps typically associated with growth. The term is inspired by quantum physics, where particles make instantaneous jumps between energy levels, symbolizing the idea of a dramatic and almost miraculous shift.

MANTRAS OF THE HIGHEST THOUGHT

I choose the path of Highest Thought and embrace the unseen realm of omnipotent possibility.

As I let go of what no longer serves me, I create space within to realize my expanded potential and welcome infinite abundance in every aspect of my life.

When I embrace the effort of seeing myself in the highest possible way, when I have the courage to reimagine who I am, who I am becoming, and what I will create, miracles of the unseen realm are natural occurrences.

Through the abundant power of praise and prayer, I now cultivate a deeper capacity to celebrate every moment on my path toward earthly happiness and spiritual joy, unaffected by worldly events and the actions or words of others.

I AM resilient, graceful, and empowered as I face life's challenges with reverence and poise, experiencing the abundant flow of life with ease and effortlessness.

I AM a Spiritual Rebel on a path of unfolding my truest self. I now welcome the loving energy of life to guide me on my unique journey.

I have unique gifts inside of me, waiting to be expressed.

Every decision I make is a valuable lesson that contributes to my growth and success. I trust that even mistakes lead to new opportunities and insights.

I trust that abundance flows to me effortlessly and that I am supported by a power greater than myself.

I release the need to control and I allow solutions to come naturally.

Regardless of my mistakes, I choose to be at peace with who I am. May all errors I've made now be transformed to serve my highest good as I release the need for approval and embrace my authentic self and unique path.

Universal abundance is the source of my good and nothing outside of myself can ever take from me what is mine by divine right.

Even when I make a mistake, I trust that I am always supported and there is a solution within reach.

When I nurture what is mine to nurture, such as my body with self-care, my children with loving affection, and my emotional wellbeing, The Universe nurtures me.

Even when external situations look and feel scary, I trust that everything is falling into place as it should because I am worthy and supported by God, The Great Creator, The Universe, The Cosmos, Pachamama (– whatever that omnipotent power is for you).

There is nowhere I AM, that God is not.

ACKNOWLEDGEMENT

I would first like to extend my heartfelt appreciation to the readers of *The Five Laws of Stillness* who are walking this path with me. Your openness to exploring new ideas and willingness to engage with this material make this experience meaningful. I hope this book serves as a beacon of light and inspiration on your own spiritual endeavors.

This book would not be possible without the help of many souls who have supported and inspired me along the way.

When I began this venture, my entire being was filled up with emotional and mental distress that had accumulated in my mind and body. I did not like who I had become and I felt uncomfortable with every aspect of myself. There are so many people that have helped me chip away the layers I've carried, simply by sharing their own light and I cannot thank you enough.

To Reverend Darlene Strickland, whose guidance I sought when I was at my lowest. Your unwavering support and ability to see my potential, and the message I needed to share, were pivotal in starting this book. To Black Crow and Grandmother Redhawk, your love and wisdom continue to strengthen my relationship with the natural world.

To the Unity of The Blue Ridge community for being a consistent space of open hearts and open minds. To Patrice Ryan, who welcomed me to help in the Unity bookstore, beginning my lifelong love for metaphysical and spiritual literature. To Jeanne Lane,

Raeus Cannon, and Cheryl Carver-Wellington, my youth group leaders, for loving me as your own child and ensuring I never missed a retreat. Big thank you to Raeus for helping me with Hebrew pronunciations on the fly. And to Jeanne, thank you for welcoming me into your life and workspace as a child.

To Finn (Evelyn Green), Laurel Hailey, and Jesse Briggs- our many adventures will forever be a cherished part of my life. To the Unity of Knoxville community, the Smiths, and Briggs family - who supported our family when we had nowhere to go and exemplified love your neighbor as yourself. I am forever thankful for the ways you showed up in our lives.

Thank you to my soul sister Christie Foley for being a constant pillar of support - the Thelma to my Louise. To Tamara Doerksen, my Rooted in Purpose podcast co-host - "It's all happening!". To all the women who have blessed me with open hearts and sacred spaces. Thank you for sharing your medicine with me. I trust that when you read this, you will feel my love and know that I am speaking to you.

Thank you to my brother Joseph, I love how you choose to see the good in situations and lend support wherever you can. To my sister Ryanne, your strength, creative power and nurturing ways have always served as inspiration to me. To my brother Steven, your ability to pave your own path and stay true to yourself is admirable and while our paths have been different, I am blessed with many memories and thankful for your place in my life.

Thank you to my dad, for always being supportive and proud of me. Thank you to my mom for following your vision to create a new way of life so your children could thrive. One of the greatest gifts you gave me was leading me to spiritual teachings that forever changed the course of my life. A cherished memory I have is seeing A Course in Miracles on your bedside table when I was a little girl.

Thank you to my husband for always having my back and my boys for being the brightest lights to enter my world. You are my greatest teachers.

I am incredibly thankful for my editor, Erin Gahan Clark. By chance, we met years before writing this book, and by synchronicity, I discovered she was an editor. You were the perfect person for this role.

Thank you to all who have contributed to the creation of this work. May we continue to seek, explore, and embrace the highest truths that resonate within us and connect us all.

Most importantly, to the Holy Spirit, Creator of All, Angels, and Ancestors that walk with me. Thank you for your guidance. Thank you for your love.

I am listening. More of this please.

ABOUT THE AUTHOR

Residing in Hendersonville, NC, Jess is a loving wife and devoted mother of two. As a business owner and entrepreneur, she balances her personal and professional pursuits with her role as a youth group leader at Unity of The Blue Ridge. She also serves as the program director for Medicine Wheel Way, a nonprofit dedicated to providing sacred space for Indigenous ceremony, celebration, and cultural preservation, with a particular focus on underserved BIPOC youth. Additionally, she is an intern water pourer and pipe carrier, committed to further deepening her spiritual understanding of Indigenous practices and ancestral connection.